ENGLISH SONNETS

English Sonnets

Edited
With Introduction and Notes
by
Sir A. T. Quiller-Couch
"Q"

NEW EDITION

Granger Poetry Library

GRANGER BOOK CO., INC.
Great Neck, N.Y.

First Published in 1897
New Edition 1935
Reprinted 1979

International Standard Book Number
0-89609-199-6

Library of Congress Catalog Number
79-51954

Printed in the United States of America

INTRODUCTION

"The Sonnet—both thing and name—comes to us from the Italian."[1] Etymologically, *sonnetto* (from *sonare*, "to play upon an instrument") is a little poem with instrumental accompaniment: just as *canzone* is a poem intended to be sung merely, and *ballata* a poem accompanied with dancing.

But as a matter of fact the earliest *sonnetti* discoverable have a proper precision of form to which the ballad and song have never yet attained, and, most likely, never will attain. We cannot trace them back beyond the thirteenth century: but the sonnets of Lodovico della Vernaccia, Pier delle Vigne, Guido Guinicelli, Jacopo da Lentino, Guittone d'Arezzo and others,[2] mostly dating between 1200 and 1250, scarcely differ in structure from the sonnet which Petrarch practised and handed down as a model to the present day. We will discuss the structure by and by.

Among these early Italians, Fra Guittone d'Arezzo—he was not a monk, but wore the prefix as a member of the half-religious, half-military

[1] Mark Pattison. Introduction to the Sonnets of John Milton.
[2] The English reader will find some account of these early Italian singers, with illustrative translations of their work, in D. G. Rossetti's *Dante and his Circle*, Part II. Poets chiefly before Dante.

INTRODUCTION

order of *Cavalieri di Santa Maria*—seems somehow
to have walked off with the credit of having per-
fected the sonnet as an instrument: insomuch that
Mr. Capel Lofft, who edited an anthology of
sonnets early in the present century,[1] salutes him as
the Columbus of poetic literature. With what justice
we are asked to prefer him above his brethren does
not quite appear. But it seems certain that he
enjoyed a great reputation in his own day, and by it
gave a certain *cachet* to the sonnet-form which he
approved and employed. Dante himself (1265-
1321), who considered Fra Guittone an over-
estimated person, uses the word "sonnet" of two
forms of composition only; and one of these, and by
far the more usual, is Guittone's form, the other
being an arrangement of two sestets followed by two
quatrains—with which we need not trouble our-
selves. Guittone's form was finally lifted and sealed
supreme by Petrarch's adoption (1304-1374), and
as the Petrarcan we may henceforth speak of it.

The Petrarcan sonnet, then, has a matter and
form of its own. In substance it is a reflective poem
on love, or at least in some mood of love. It has a
unity of its own, and must be the expression of a
single thought or feeling. In structure it obeys the
following rules:

1. It consists of fourteen lines, each line having
five beats or musical stresses.

[1] Capel Lofft, *Laura*, 1813-1814.

INTRODUCTION

2. The lines must rhyme: and in the disposition of its rhymes the sonnet divides into two systems, the first eight lines forming the major system and the remaining six the minor.

The major system of eight lines, or two quatrains, is called the octave: the minor system of six lines, or two tercets, is called the sestet.

3. The octave must contain two rhyme-sounds only: and although in some Petrarcan sonnets we find these arranged in simple alternation (A B, A B, A B, A B), in an octave of the normal type lines 1, 4, 5, 8 will rhyme together, and lines 2, 3, 6, 7 will rhyme together upon a different note (A B B A, A B B A).

4. The sestet may contain either two or three rhyme-sounds: but none of these must repeat or resemble the rhyme-sounds of the octave. And some hold that, to be perfectly normal, the sestet should have the division between its tercets clearly marked: thus e.g. we may have C D C, D C D, or C D E, C D E, besides other variations.

5. In expressing what the poet has to say, the sonnet must adopt itself to the intention of its length or structure. The octave should present the poet's idea, the sestet apply it: or the octave should introduce and develop an image, the sestet give back the general reflection suggested by it. In either case there will be a marked pause between the two.

INTRODUCTION

Besides this indispensable pause, there should be—
we may take it as a counsel of perfection and a rule
subject to many conditions of expediency—two
lesser pauses; the first between the two quatrains of
the octave, the second between the two tercets of the
sestet. Thus a Petrarcan sonnet ordered upon a
Platonic idea of perfection—upon a model "laid up
somewhere in the heavens"—would run somewhat as
follows: The first quatrain *introduces* the poet's
thought or mood, after a slight pause, "as of one who
is turning over what has been said in the mind to
enforce it further," the second quatrain *develops* it:
then, after a deep pause, the minor system opens, and
the first tercet takes up the thought and *applies* it or
reveals a deeper suggestiveness; and the concluding
tercet *sums up* the whole matter in a general reflection.

Such then was the Petrarcan sonnet in matter and
form; and such in matter and form (subject to
minor experiments and variations) the sonnet re-
mained in the hands of Michael Angelo, Tasso, and
the great Italians; of Camoens; and of Ronsard,
Du Bellay and the early French sonneteers.

The first English sonnets appeared in the year
1557, in the book commonly known as *Tottel's
Miscellany*. It had for its formal title "Songes and
sonnettes written by the ryght honorable lorde
Henry Howard, late earle of Surrey and other": and
was in fact the first and posthumous edition of the
poems of the Earl of Surrey and Sir Thomas Wyat,
with other pieces by contemporaries named and

unnamed. The editor, Nicholas Grimald (whose name suggests Grimaldi and an Italian parentage[1]), avows the source of his poets' inspiration, and hopes by their experiments to prove that "the English tongue can earn like praise with the Italian and other." *Tottel's Miscellany* marks the opening of an epoch in the history of English song—an epoch of Italian influence which lasted for more than a century, and was not fairly superseded by the influence of France until the Restoration. Wyat and Surrey together brought the sonnet into England: nor can we say positively of this pair that one gave a lead to the other. But if one must have the credit, the probabilities favour Wyat. He was the elder: he had spent some time in Italy, which Surrey never visited: and he keeps more closely by the Petrarcan model, from which the sonnets of Surrey diverge, and on lines which subsequent Elizabethan poets steadily widened.

For these English experimenters, while constant to the Petrarcan tradition that in substance the sonnet should be a short reflective poem on love, in structure allowed themselves a licence of innovation which gradually evolved a type so unlike the Petrarcan that some critics have believed it a plant of independent growth, indigenous to our island.[2] Others, such as the late Mr. Mark Pattison, will have nothing to do with it, and go so far as to declare that

[1] Professor Henry Morley, *English Writers*, Vol. VIII, pp. 51-52.
[2] This theory was advanced by Mr. Hall Caine, *Sonnets of Three Centuries*.

INTRODUCTION

the immortal sonnets of Shakespeare (written on this model) are "not sonnets at all"!—the aim of such criticism being apparently the composite one of vindicating pedantry on the one hand and saving expense of labour on the other. "If it had been recognised," says Mr. Pattison, "that the so-called sonnets of Shakespeare are not sonnets at all, any more than those of Lord Brooke, but a continuous poem, or poems, written in fourteen-line stanzas, as Tennyson's *In Memoriam* is, largely, in sixteen-line stanzas, how much misplaced skill would have been saved!" It is usually possible to save yourself trouble by considering something as something else, especially if you thereby remove it from the category of things you happen to be studying into the category of things on which you propose to bestow no attention: but that you serve the interests of sound criticism by this process seems disputable; and yet more disputable when you ignore an author's plain intention. One solid reason (among many) why the Sonnets of Shakespeare are sonnets, while the stanzas of *In Memoriam* are not, is that Shakespeare was endeavouring to write sonnets, and Tennyson was endeavouring to do nothing of the sort.

On the evolution of this Shakespearian type we may say a few words. Wyat observed generally the Petrarcan form in the two opening quatrains (A B B A, A B B A), and the Petrarcan use of three rhymes in the second part of the sonnet: but he did not observe Petrarch's avoidance of couplets in the second part. He closed every sonnet with a couplet, and this innovation had far-reaching results. Surrey, in the ardour of experiment, attempted many different arrangements of rhyme, but always closed with a couplet; and to this conclusion Spenser was equally loyal. Its expressive value (and it has great expressive value, deny it who will) effaced for a time, in the appreciation of our poets, the more subtly expressive value of the octave and sestet, with their pauses. These vanished as it grew more and more the main business of the sonnet to lead up to a couplet which clinched, as it were, the thought of the preceding lines with something of an epigrammatic stroke: until we find the structure of Surrey's loosest experiments adopted by Daniel and Shakespeare as the final type of English sonnet—the easy form of four quatrains and a couplet all independently rhymed.

But not even Shakespeare could make the genius of our language content with this form. More learned poets—Ben Jonson in his Sonnet to the Lady Mary Worth, Donne (whose fine Sonnet to Death will be found on p. 77), and Drummond of Hawthornden—soon reverted to the Petrarcan octave for its superior neatness: and Drummond, especially, composed sonnets in large numbers (mostly translations or imitations) which might fairly be called Petrarcan but for their final couplets. No English writer could yet find it in his heart to end the sonnet otherwise.

INTRODUCTION

Here are the two forms for comparison:

Petrarcan			Shakespearian		
A	⎫		A	⎫	
B	⎬		B	⎬ 1	
B	⎬ Octave	A	⎬	
A	⎭		B	⎭	
A	⎫		C	⎫	
B	⎬		D	⎬ 2	Quatrains
B			C	⎬	
A			D	⎭	
C	⎫		E	⎫	
D	⎬		F	⎬ 3	
E	⎭ Sestet		E	⎬	
			F	⎭	
C	⎫		G	⎫ Couplet	
D	⎬		G	⎭	
E	⎭				

Petrarcan in substance it had always remained—
an exercise upon the theme of love, usually of hope-
less or unsuccessful love: and the theme had fairly
exhausted itself in sugared and artificial conceits,
when a great poet arose and reformed the English
sonnet in substance as well as structure.

Milton—scholar that he was—recognised the
beauty of the Petrarcan type and revived its rhyme-

INTRODUCTION

arrangement, octave and sestet, with this difference —*he obliterated the pauses*. A Miltonic sonnet sweeps from opening to close without a break; it glows "as if he had cut his diamond in such a way that only one luminous light was visible to us": or again, "he considered—so we may infer—that the English sonnet should be like a revolving sphere, every portion becoming continuously visible, with no break in the continuity of thought or expression anywhere apparent."[1] In one example only—that addressed to Cromwell—did he admit the final couplet. For a true specimen of the noble impetuous Miltonic movement the reader should study the famous "Avenge, O Lord, thy slaughtered saints. . . ."

But his great and enduring reform was one of substance. To each one of the poets who became colleagues in the Latin Secretaryship under the Protectorate there seems to have come the desire to discover some English vehicle for the Horatian Ode —that singular product so much easier to recognise than describe. Marvel attempted and scored one great success. I refer, of course, to his *Horatian Ode upon Cromwell's Return from Ireland*, and may quote again the often quoted lines on Charles's execution, to exemplify its spirit and its stanzas:

[1] Mr. William Sharp, *The Sonnet*, prefixed to his *Sonnets of This Century*.

INTRODUCTION

"He nothing common did, or mean,
　Upon that memorable scene,
　　But with his keener eye
　　The axe's edge did try;
　Nor called the gods with vulgar spite
　To vindicate his helpless night;
　　But bowed his comely head
　　Down as upon a bed."

Though a success, it had no progeny. Milton, steering wider of Horace's Alcaics, chose a verse-form ready to his hand—the Sonnet. "If," says Mr. Robert Bridges,[1] "we compare, for example, his *Cyriack, whose grandsire,* with *Martiis cœlebs* or *Æli vetusto,* there can be no doubt that Milton was here deliberately using the sonnet form to do the work of Horace's tight stanzas; and not the whole of Shakespeare's or Petrarch's sonnets set alongside will show enough kinship with these sonnets of Milton to draw them away from their affinity with Horace."

But, like many another great artist, Milton carried his experiment to issues far beyond his original aim. His sonnets were no chamber exercises: each owed its inspiration to a real occasion, and that inspiration of reality lifted it high above mere simulation of the Horatian mode. "Each person, thing, or fact is a moment in Milton's life on which he was stirred; sometimes in the soul's depths, some-

[1] *Essay on Keats,* printed as a Critical Introduction to the Poems of Keats, edited by G. Thorn Drury.

times on the surface of feeling, but always truly moved. . . . It is a man who is speaking to us, not an artist attitudinising to please us."[1]

"In his hand
The Thing became a Trumpet whence he blew
Soul-animating strains——"

And when, after a slumber of a hundred years, the sonnet awoke again in England, it awoke with Milton's seal on its brow. Wordsworth narrates that "in the cottage, Town-end, Grasmere, one afternoon in 1801, my sister read to me the Sonnets of Milton. I had long been well acquainted with them, but I was particularly struck on that occasion with the dignified simplicity and harmony that runs through most of them,—in character so different from the Italian, and still more so from Shakespeare's fine Sonnets. I took fire, if I may be allowed to say so, and produced three sonnets the same afternoon, the first I ever wrote except an irregular one at school."[2]

Shakespeare, Milton, Wordsworth, Keats, Rossetti, Mrs. Browning—these are confessedly the great sonneteers of our language; and though all will not agree in accounting Wordsworth the greatest, few will deny that his finest sonnets were harder to spare than any other's finest. They combine the reality,

[1] Mark Pattison.
[2] The irregular sonnet referred to, page 115 in our collection, "Calm is all nature as a resting wheel . . ." Written, perhaps, as early as 1786.

the "alive-ness" of Milton's with a more general and more permanent applicability: their verity is universal, and appeals to the conscience of all men. It is given to few to take more than an historical interest in the question of parochial endowment and others which agitated the Long Parliament. Only the initiated will listen with entire patience (because with understanding) to the *arcana* of love as uttered by Shakespeare and Rossetti; or sympathise with the languors of Keats, or with the passionate doubts of Mrs. Browning. But dull indeed would he be of soul who could pass by such a sonnet as Wordsworth's "The world is too much with us . . ." or his valedictory sonnet to Duddon, with its immortal close. "To find," says Mr. John Morley,[1] "beautiful and pathetic language, set to harmonious numbers, for the common impressions of meditative minds, is no small part of the poet's task." It was the part which Wordsworth performed to perfection. His poetry, as Johnson said of Gray's Elegy, "abounds with images which find a mirror in every mind, and with sentiments to which every bosom returns an echo." "I never before," records George Eliot, "met with so many of my own feelings expressed just as I should like them." On the response of the common conscience of men Wordsworth's sonnets may rely for their perpetual justification.

For his form Wordsworth went back to the true

[1] Introduction to the Complete Poetical Works of William Wordsworth, 1893.

INTRODUCTION

Petrarcan, reintroducing the pause which Milton had slurred, and reassigning to the octave and sestet their proper functions. By the favour of such artists as Mrs. Browning, Dante Gabriel Rossetti, Christina Rossetti, Mr. Swinburne, Mr. William Watson, Mr. Watts-Dunton, Mr. Gosse, and Mr. Andrew Lang, and by all but unanimous consent of the critics, the Petrarcan form has ever since retained its pride of place. Keats to be sure (whose sonnets some lovers of poetry rank next to Shakespeare's; though on what ground it is hard to see) provides the dissentients with a sorely needed support; almost all his early sonnets being Petrarcan in system and all his later ones Shakespearian. But the deliberate reversion of one poet, even of Keats's quality, cannot seriously shake the great mass of modern authority.

It is customary for those who write on this subject to give rules by which a good sonnet may be constructed. But our aim here is not to assist the reader in this or any form of composition. The sonnet has immense popularity just at present, among versifiers. Critics, on the other hand, begin to discover impatience with a form capable of enshrining so much verse of which one can only say, with Charles Lamb, "it discovers much tender feeling; it is most like Petrarch of any foreign Poet, or what we might have supposed Petrarch would have written if Petrarch had been born a fool!" It is hoped that a small volume containing specimens of the best English sonnet-writing of the past will provide the reader

INTRODUCTION

with a corrective and a touch-stone of taste. Certainly the study of these specimens ought to assure him that the Sonnet is no arbitrary or haphazard invention; that its length and its peculiar structure were not fixed on by chance; but that every rule has its reason; and that (in a phrase which I may be allowed to repeat) it is the men big enough to break the rules who accept and observe them most cheerfully.

A. T. QUILLER-COUCH

1897

PREFACE TO THIS EDITION

The aim of the above Introduction, written some thirty-eight years ago, scarcely reached beyond a simple exposition of the sonnet-form and its rules as observed or modified by various English poets; and in the exposition, so far as it went, I find little that I should now put otherwise.

The original selection, however, ended with Mrs. Browning's *Sonnets from the Portuguese*—it may be because the publishers in those days felt shy of letting loose an untried anthologist upon copyright matter. Or perhaps he chose his exhibits, too academically, for their differences, as illustrating his argument, rather than with strict consideration of their degrees of merit as poetry, and supposed he had presented enough for his purpose. At any rate, by the publishers' favour and that of a faithful if attenuated line of purchasers, the book has been kept alive; and now, continuing my anthology to the present day, I must needs take account of the pre-vailing attitude of our present-day poets towards the sonnet in practice, as well as of some critical theories about it unknown to me in 1897.

In 1897, then—its distance back in time may be realised by recalling that it was the year of Queen Victoria's Jubilee—death had quenched the star

PREFACE TO THIS EDITION

poets and prophets of their time—Browning, Tennyson, Rossetti, Morris, Carlyle, Ruskin; and the young of the 'nineties consoled themselves with a passion of craze for "form," in part (as I remember) traceable to France and a sympathetic admiration for France as, largely through the compelling power of her writers and painters, she had risen again to her queenly stature from the abasement of 1870. One has but to run over a list—Dobson, Lang, Henley, Wilde, Dowson and other experimenters in sonnet, roundel, ballade, villanelle, triolet, etc.—to realise their common preoccupation with forms and shapes of verse.

Now of all these shapes the Sonnet, if only by virtue of its lineage in our literature, held the immeasurably greatest prestige. Rondeaux and villanelles might be French, and toys: but the Sonnet, naturalised by our greatest practitioners, was now as English as the oak or the rose. All could grow the flower, given fourteen lines for its scanty plot of ground and a few elementary rules: the consequence quickly apparent in an epidemic of sonneteering on any and every subject by indifferent versifiers, with whose output it will be noted that my "Introduction" betrayed some impatience at the time. Mostly, as one remembers, it raged its course in and around the Lake District, having Wordsworth for its excuse. Beyond cavil Wordsworth within his fertile period achieved some, and not a few, of the greatest sonnets in our language. But as Lowell wrote shrewdly:—

PREFACE TO THIS EDITION

"Wordsworth was dimly conscious of (his besetting prolixity) and turned by a kind of instinct, I suspect, to the Sonnet, because its form forced boundaries upon him and put him under bonds to hold his peace at the end of the fourteenth line. Yet even here Nature would out, and the oft-recurring 'Same Subject Continued' lures the Nun from her cell to the convent parlour, and tempts the student to make a pulpit of his pensive citadel. The hour-glass is there to be sure, with its lapsing admonition. But it reminds the preacher only that it can be turned."

At his best the poet of "Westminster Bridge," "The Extinction of the Venetian Republic," "The world is too much with us" was admittedly magnificent; but these are self-contained sonnets and obey rules of structure. In "Toussaint l'Ouverture," "O friend! I know not . . .," the "Valedictory to Duddon" he followed Milton's innovation of running the octave into the sestet with *enjambement* and a sharp cæsura early in the ninth line: and the trick is effective, though priests condemn it.[1] But these fine sonnets, again, are "self-contained." Each opens and closes a single sentiment or reflection. In sum, Wordsworth put himself to school and did wonders so long as he kept himself there; then self-

[1] Mrs. Browning employs it habitually in *Sonnets from the Portuguese*. I suspect that she took it from Wordsworth. The device, so far as I know, was not used by the Portuguese—by Camoens, for example.

complacency and his natural verbosity overcame him; he felt sure that he could write a sonnet without effort on any subject, and as a result we have not only the dreary waste of his *Ecclesiastical Sonnets* and *Sonnets Upon the Punishment of Death* ("Snore, heavenly Muse!") but an endless desert of undistinguished fourteen-liners by imitators of Wordsworth's diction—Time's revenge upon the author of the famous Prefaces to *Lyrical Ballads!*

But this raises a question more general than Wordsworth's own default in "slop-over," or the tediousness of his disciples—which is: If the ideal Sonnet be this absolute complete-in-itself thing, what are we to say about sonnet-sequences? The late Mr. T. W. H. Crosland, a sensitive critic and an upholder of the complete-in-itself doctrine, had to face (in his treatise *The English Sonnet*, 1926) his doctrine's difficulty with history—that "historically the sonnet may be said almost to have its foundation in the sequence. The sonneteers down to Shakespeare wrote sequences and nothing but sequences"; and the body of Shakespeare's *Sonnets*, as it has come to us, is obviously a patchwork of unrelated sequences, *disjecta membra*. Mr. Crosland, allowing for this, and for some admired sequences by modern poets, did not hesitate over his own conclusion:—

"Broadly, therefore, we shall pronounce the sonnet sequence, considered as a complete work of itself, to be technically vicious and undesirable.

PREFACE TO THIS EDITION

In the modern sonnet, at any rate, its tendency is
to introduce violations of the sonnet law which
are distressing and ought not to be tolerated. The
poet who writes two sonnets in sequence is tacitly
admitting that his first flight has failed, and that his
emotion or passion has not been brought to its
proper focus."

And if the poet answer that, on the contrary, his
subject has so moved and uplifted him that he over-
flows and produces two sonnets instead of one,
Mr. Crosland has his reply ready, that—

"he has not really written two sonnets, but a poem
in two fourteen-line stanzas; which, inasmuch as
the stanzas are of a form which peculiarly suggest
the sonnet, fail not only as sonnets but as stanzas.
This is no arbitrary judgement, but will be found
to have its justification in poetic, and in formal
and melodic law."

If this be no arbitrary judgement it looks suspiciously
like one, and suspiciously like the error of Castel-
vetro, who constructed "laws" of dramatic unity
partly on a misreading of Aristotle and mostly out
of his own head. Mr. Crosland's argument through-
out, indeed, would seem to personify the Sonnet as
of itself a legislative dictator. It seems to me (habitu-
ally distrustful of notional personifications) enough
to say that for a short poem expressive of a single
thought or emotion Petrarch wedded a perfect

length with a structure fitting it so admirably as to be tampered with only at a grave risk; but that the risk has often been dared and successfully. Concerning sequences, however, let me concede, as a matter of personal taste, that a sonnet-sequence is apt to bore me soonest of all forms of poetry; demanding to be taken "at long breath," and, seeking a reason for this—and while disclaiming any purpose to instruct —I find a hint that may be worth the reader's weighing. In an Eastern *Gazal* (by Hafiz, for example), though the form be severe, there is no strict connection of thought—certainly no *obvious* connection between the distichs. The skill of it, often amazing, lies rather in bringing together a number of separate images so that they form in the end a pattern and leave a general and beautiful impression. One may call it an exquisite art of saying a thing without saying it in so many words. But I have not knowledge enough to suggest more than a hint, and that diffidently.

The hint, however, may convey my belief that the sonnet has possibilities of development in form, and my real joy at watching its revival of late in the practice of young poets, after an interval during which a very few—and of these Lord Alfred Douglas most signally—have kept its fine tradition alive.[1] It went out of vogue largely through a surfeit of inferior

[1] The few modern sonnets which end this collection (beginning with Hopkins) are added to indicate some lines on which the Sonnet may yet develop. I hope: but my trade is not with prophecy.

PREFACE TO THIS EDITION

stuff, aggravating the general post-war tendency against "form" and in favour of "content." Well, as for "content" or "subject," its whole history, from the Petrarcan theme of frustrated love to Milton's "trumpet" and Wordsworth's morality, should be augury against doubt of an elastic future. It is a lovely form to fit and hold lovely thoughts. It must not, however, be stretched to be compared uncritically, as some have done, in difficulty or impressiveness, with drama or epic, things of magnitude.

Q.

The Haven
Fowey, Cornwall
August 20th, 1935

ACKNOWLEDGMENT

My thanks, for permission to include certain copyright material in this anthology, are due to Lord Alfred Douglas and The Poet Laureate; to Lady Watson and Mrs. Thomas Hardy; to the Executors of Wilfrid Blunt, Gerard Manley Hopkins, Rupert Brooke and Wilfred Owen; and, for an unpublished sonnet, to my friend Robert Gittings.

ENGLISH SONNETS

SIR THOMAS WYATT
[*circ.* 1503-1542]

The Hind

Whoso list to hunt, I know where is an hind,
  But as for me, *helas!* I may no more.
  The vain travail hath wearied me so sore,
I am of them that furthest come behind.
Yet may I, by no means, my wearied mind
  Draw from the deer; but as she fleeth afore
  Fainting I follow. I leave off therefore,
Since in a net I seek to hold the wind.
Who list her hunt, I put him out of doubt,
  As well as I, may spend his time in vain;
  And graven with diamonds in letters plain
There is written, her fair neck round about,
    "*Noli me tangere*, for Caesar's I am,
    And wild for to hold, though I seem tame."

HENRY HOWARD, EARL OF SURREY
[?1517-1546-7]

Description of Spring: Wherein each thing renews, save only the Lover

THE soote season, that bud and bloom furth brings,
 With green hath clad the hill and eke the vale,
The nightingale with feathers new she sings;
 The turtle to her mate hath told her tale.
Summer is come, for every spray now springs,
 The hart hath hung his old head on the pale;
The buck in brake his winter coat he flings;
 The fishes flete with new repairèd scale;
The adder all her slough away she slings;
 The swift swallow pursueth the flies smale;
The busy bee her honey now she mings;
 Winter is worn that was the flowers' bale.
  And thus I see among these pleasant things
  Each care decays, and yet my sorrow springs.

HENRY HOWARD, EARL OF SURREY

A Vow to Love Faithfully, Howsoever he be Rewarded

SET me whereas the sun doth parch the green,
  Or where his beams do not dissolve the ice:
In temperate heat, where he is felt and seen;
  In presence prest of people mad or wise;
Set me in high, or yet in low degree;
  In longest night, or in the shortest day;
In clearest sky, or where clouds thickest be;
  In lusty youth, or when my hairs be gray:
Set me in heaven, in earth, or else in hell,
  In hill, or dale, or in the foaming flood;
Thrall, or at large, alive whereso I dwell,
  Sick, or in health, in evil fame, or good;
    Hers will I be; and with this only thought
    Content myself, although my hap be nought.

HENRY HOWARD, EARL OF SURREY

The Cornet[1]

I NEVER saw you, madam, lay apart
   Your cornet black, in cold nor yet in heat,
   Sith first ye knew of my desire so great,
Which other fancies chased clean from my heart.
Whiles to my self I did the thought reserve,
   That so unware did wound my woeful breast,
   Pity I saw within your heart did rest.
But since ye knew I did you love and serve,
Your golden tress was clad alway in black,
   Your smiling looks were hid thus evermore,
   All that withdrawn that I did crave so sore.
So doth this cornet govern me, alack!
      In summer's sun, in winter breath of frost,
      Of your fair eyes whereby the light is lost.

[1] Cornet: a tall head-dress, shaped like an inverted horn.

4

SIR EDWARD DYER

[*circ.* 1540-1607]

The Shepherd's Conceit of Prometheus

PROMETHEUS, when first from heaven high
  He brought down fire, ere then on earth unseen,
Fond of the light, a satyr, standing by,
  Gave it a kiss, as it like sweet had been.
Feeling forthwith the other's burning power,
  Wood[1] with the smart, with shouts and shriekings
      shrill,
He sought his ease in river, field and bower,
  But for the time his grief went with him still.
So silly I, with that unwonted sight,
  In human shape an angel from above,
Feeding mine eyes, th' impression there did light,
  That since I run and rest as pleaseth Love.
    The difference is, the satyr's lips, my heart,—
    He for a while, I evermore have smart.

[1] Wild.

5

SIR WALTER RALEIGH
[1552-1618]

A Vision upon the Faery Queen

METHOUGHT I saw the grave where Laura lay,
    Within that temple where the vestal flame
Was wont to burn; and passing by that way
    To see that buried dust of living fame,
Whose tomb fair Love and fairer Virtue kept,
    All suddenly I saw the Faery Queen:
At whose approach the soul of Petrarch wept;
    And from thenceforth those Graces were not seen,
For they this Queen attended; in whose stead
    Oblivion laid him down on Laura's hearse.
Hereat the hardest stones were seen to bleed,
    And groans of buried ghosts the heavens did pierce,
      Where Homer's spright did tremble all for grief,
      And cursed the accéss of that celestial thief.

EDMUND SPENSER
[1553-1598]

To His Book

HAPPY ye leaves whenas those lily hands,
  Which hold my life in their dead-doing might,
Shall handle you, and hold in love's soft bands,
  Like captives trembling at the victor's sight:
  And happy lines, on which with starry light
Those lamping eyes will deign sometime to look
  And read the sorrows of my dying sprite,
Written with tears in heart's close bleeding book:
And happy rhymes, bathed in the sacred brook
  Of *Helicon*, whence she derivèd is,
When ye behold that angel's blessèd look,
  My soul's long lackèd food, my heaven's bliss:
    Leaves, lines, and rhymes, seek her to please
    alone,
    Whom if ye please, I care for other none.

EDMUND SPENSER

The Cuckoo

THE merry Cuckoo, messenger of Spring,
  His trumpet shrill hath thrice already sounded;
That warns all lovers wait upon their king,
  Who now is coming forth with garland crownèd.
  With noise whereof the choir of birds resounded
Their anthems sweet devisèd of Love's praise;
  That all the woods their echoes back rebounded,
As if they knew the meaning of their lays.
But 'mongst them all which did Love's honour raise,
  No word was heard of her that most it ought:
But she his precept idly disobeys,
  And doth his idle message set at nought.
    Therefore, O Love, unless she turn to thee,
    Ere Cuckoo end, let her a rebel be!

EDMUND SPENSER

The Summons

FRESH Spring, the herald of Love's mighty King,
   In whose cote-armour richly are display'd
All sorts of flowers the which on earth do spring
   In goodly colours gloriously array'd,—
   Go to my Love, where she is careless laid
Yet in her Winter's bower not well awake:
   Tell her the joyous time will not be stay'd
Unless she do him by the fore-lock take:
Bid her therefore herself soon ready make:
   To wait on Love amongst his lovely crew:
Where every one that misseth then her make,[1]
   Shall be by him amerced with penance due.
     Make haste therefore, sweet Love, whilst it is
      prime,
     For none can call again the passèd time.

[1] Mate.

EDMUND SPENSER

April Smile

MARK when she smiles with amiable cheer,
  And tell me whereto can ye liken it—
When on each eyelid sweetly do appear
  An hundred Graces as in shade to sit?
  Likest it seemeth to my simple wit
Unto the fair sunshine in summer's day,
  That, when a dreadful storm away is flit,
Through the broad world doth spread his goodly ray:
At sight whereof each bird that sits on spray,
  And every beast that to his den was fled,
Comes forth afresh out of their late dismay,
  And to the light lift up their drooping head.
    So my storm-beaten heart likewise is cheer'd
    With that sunshine when cloudy looks are clear'd.

EDMUND SPENSER

The Star His Guide

LIKE as a ship that through the ocean wide,
  By conduct of some star, doth make her way,
Whenas a storm hath dimmed her trusty guide,
  Out of her course doth wander far astray,—
  So I, whose star, that wont with her bright ray
Me to direct, with clouds is overcast,
  Do wander now, in darkness and dismay,
Through hidden perils round about me placed;
Yet hope I well that, when this storm is past,
  My Helice,[1] the lodestar of my life,
Will shine again, and look on me at last,
  With lovely light to clear my cloudy grief.
    Till then I wander careful, comfortless,
    In secret sorrow and sad pensiveness.

[1] Helice, or Callisto, daughter of Lycaon, King of Arcadia, was beloved of Zeus, and by the jealousy of Hera transformed into a she-bear; wherefrom Zeus again transformed her into a constellation, the "Great Bear".

EDMUND SPENSER

Her Surrender

LIKE as a huntsman after weary chase,
  Seeing the game from him escaped away,
Sits down to rest him in some shady place,
  With panting hounds beguilèd of their prey:
  So, after long pursuit and vain assay,
When I all weary had the chase forsook,
  The gentle deer returned the self-same way,
Thinking to quench her thirst at the next brook.
There she beholding me with milder look,
  Sought not to fly, but fearless still did bide,
Till I in hand her yet half-trembling took,
  And with her own good will her firmly tied.
    Strange things meseemed, to see a beast so wild
    So goodly won, with her own will beguiled!

EDMUND SPENSER

Widowed

LIKE as the Culver[1] on the barèd bough
  Sits mourning for the absence of her mate;
And in her song sends many a wishful vow
  For his return that seems to linger late.
  So I alone now left disconsolate
Mourn to myself the absence of my love:
  And wand'ring here and there all desolate
Seek with my plaints to match that mournful dove.
Ne joy of aught that under heaven doth hove
  Can comfort me, but her own joyous sight
Whose sweet aspect both God and man can move
  In her unspotted pleasance to delight.
    Dark is my day whiles her fair light I miss,
    And dead my life that wants such lively bliss.

[1] Dove.

EDMUND SPENSER

FAIR Proud! now tell me, why should fair be proud?
　　Sith all world's glory is but dross unclean,
And in the shade of death itself shall shroud,
　　However now thereof ye little ween!
　　That goodly idol, now so gay beseen,
Shall doff her flesh's borrowed fair attire,
　　And be forgot as it had never been,
That many now much worship and admire!
Ne any then shall after it inquire,
　　Ne any mention shall thereof remain,
But what this verse, that never shall expire,
　　Shall to you purchase, with her thankless pain.
　　　　Fair! be no longer proud of that 'shall perish;
　　　　But that which shall you make immortal cherish.

EDMUND SPENSER

Kilcoran Strand

ONE day I wrote her name upon the strand,
　But came the waves and washèd it away:
Again I wrote it with a second hand,
　But came the tide and made my pains his prey.
　Vain man (said she), that dost in vain assay
A mortal thing so to immortalise;
　For I myself shall like to this decay,
And eke my name be wipèd out likewise.
Not so (quod I); let baser things devise
　To die in dust, but you shall live by fame;
My verse your virtues rare shall eternise,
　And in the heavens write your glorious name:
　　Where, whenas Death shall all the world subdue,
　　Our love shall live, and later life renew.

EDMUND SPENSER

Lent

This holy season, fit to fast and pray,
   Men to devotion ought to be inclined:
Therefore I likewise on so holy day
   For my sweet Saint some service fit will find.
   Her temple fair is built within my mind,
In which her glorious image placèd is,
   On which my thoughts do day and night attend,
Like sacred priests that never think amiss!
There I to her, as the author of my bliss,
   Will build an altar to appease her ire,
And on the same my heart will sacrifice,
   Burning in flames of pure and chaste desire:
     The which vouchsafe O Goddess! to accept,
     Amongst thy dearest relics to be kept.

EDMUND SPENSER

Easter

MOST glorious Lord of life! that on this day
  Didst make thy triumph over death and sin,
And having harrowed hell didst bring away
  Captivity thence captive, us to win:
  This joyous day, dear Lord, with joy begin;
And grant that we, for whom Thou diddest die,
  Being with thy dear blood clean washed from sin,
May live for ever in felicity,
And that thy love we weighing worthily,
  May likewise love Thee for the same again;
And for thy sake, that all like dear didst buy,
  With love may one another entertain.
    So let us love, dear Love, like as we ought:
    Love is the lesson which the Lord us taught.

JOHN FLORIO
[1553-1625]

Concerning the Honour of Books

SINCE honour from the honourer proceeds,
  How well do they deserve that memorize
  And leave in Books for all posterities
The names of worthies and their virtuous deeds:
When all their glory else, like water-weeds
  Without their element, preséntly dies,
  And all their greatness quite forgotten lies,
And when and how they flourished no man heeds!
How poor remembrances are statues, tombs,
  And other monuments that men erect
To princes, which remain in closèd rooms
  Where but a few behold them, in respect
    Of Books, that to the universal eye
    Show how they lived; the other where they lie!

SIR PHILIP SIDNEY
[1554-1586]

Against Artifice

You that do search for every purling spring
   Which from the ribs of old Parnassus flows,
   And every flower, not sweet perhaps, which grows
Near thereabouts into your poesy wring;
You that do dictionary's method bring
   Into your rhymes, running in rattling rows;
   You that poor Petrarch's long deceased woes
With new-born sighs and denizened wit do sing;
You take wrong ways; those far-fet helps be such
As do bewray a want of inward touch,
   And sure at length stolen goods do come to light.
But if, both for your love and skill, your name
You seek to nurse at fullest breasts of Fame,
   Stella behold, and then begin to indite.

SIR PHILIP SIDNEY

The Moon

WITH how sad steps, O Moon! thou climb'st the skies!
  How silently, and with how wan a face!
  What! may it be that even in heavenly place
That busy archer his sharp arrows tries?
Sure, if that long-with-love-acquainted eyes
  Can judge of love, thou feel'st a lover's case;
  I read it in thy looks: thy languished grace,
To me, that feel the like, thy state descries.
Then, even of fellowship, O Moon! tell me,
  Is constant love deemed there but want of wit?
Are beauties there as proud as here they be?
  Do they above love to be loved, and yet
    Those lovers scorn whom that love doth possess?—
  Do they call "virtue" there ungratefulness?

SIR PHILIP SIDNEY

Sleep

COME, Sleep, O Sleep! the certain knot of peace,
  The baiting-place of wit, the balm of woe,
The poor man's wealth, the prisoner's release,
  The indifferent judge between the high and low;
With shield of proof shield me from out the prease
  Of those fierce darts Despair at me doth throw:
Oh, make in me those civil wars to cease!
  I will good tribute pay if thou do so.
Take thou of me smooth pillows, sweetest bed,
  A chamber deaf to noise and blind of light,
A rosy garland and a weary head:
  And if these things, as being thine by right,
    Move not thy heavy grace, thou shalt in me
    Livelier than elsewhere Stella's image see.

SIR PHILIP SIDNEY

The Lists

HAVING this day my horse, my hand, my lance
  Guided so well that I obtained the prize,
  Both by the judgement of the English eyes
And of some sent from that sweet enemy, France;
Horsemen my skill in horsemanship advance,
  Town-folks my strength; a daintier judge applies
  His praise to sleight which from good use doth rise;
Some lucky wits impute it but to chance;
Others, because of both sides I do take
  My blood from them who did excel in this,
Think Nature me a man of arms did make.
  How far they shot awry! The true cause is,
    Stella looked on, and from her heavenly face
    Sent forth the beams which made so fair my
    race.

SIR PHILIP SIDNEY

The Road

HIGHWAY! since you my chief Parnassus be,
  And that my Muse, to some ears not unsweet,
  Tempers her words to trampling horses' feet
More oft than to a chamber melody,—
Now blessèd you, bear onward blessèd me
  To her, where I my heart, safe-left, shall meet;
  My Muse and I must you of duty greet,
With thanks and wishes, wishing thankfully.
Be you still fair, honoured by public heed,
  By no encroachment wronged, nor time forgot,
Nor blamed for blood, nor shamed for sinful deed,
  And that you know I envy you no lot
    Of highest wish, I wish you so much bliss,
    Hundreds of years you Stella's feet may kiss!

SIR PHILIP SIDNEY

Friendship

My true love hath my heart, and I have his,
  By just exchange one for the other given;
I hold his dear, and mine he cannot miss;
  There never was a better bargain driven.
His heart in me keeps me and him in one;
  My heart in him his thoughts and senses guides;
He loves my heart, for once it was his own;
  I cherish his, because in me it bides.
His heart his wound receivèd from my sight;
  My heart was wounded with his wounded heart:
For as from me on him his hurt did light,
  So still methought in me his hurt did smart.
    Both equal hurt, in this change sought one bliss:
    My true love hath my heart, and I have his.

SIR PHILIP SIDNEY

Splendidis Longum Valedico Nugis

LEAVE me, O Love, which reachest but to dust,
  And thou, my mind, aspire to higher things!
Grow rich in that which never taketh rust:
  Whatever fades but fading pleasure brings.
Draw in thy beams, and humble all thy might
  To that sweet yoke where lasting freedoms be,
Which breaks the clouds and opens forth the light
  That doth both shine and give us sight to see.
Oh, take fast hold! let that light be thy guide
  In this small course which birth draws out to
    death,
And think how evil becometh him to slide
  Who seeketh heaven, and comes of heavenly
    breath.
    Then farewell, world! thy uttermost I see:
    Eternal Love, maintain thy life in me!

FULKE GREVILLE, LORD BROOKE
[1554-1628]

To Cupid

Cupid, thou naughty boy, when thou wert loathèd,
  Naked and blind, for vagabonding noted,
Thy nakedness I with my Reason clothèd,
  Mine eyes I gave thee—so was I devoted.
Fie, wanton, fie! Who would show children kindness?
  No sooner he into mine eyes was gotten
But straight he clouds them with a seeming blindness,
  Makes Reason wish that Reason were forgotten.
From thence to Myra's eyes the wanton strayeth,
  Where, while I charge him with ungrateful
    measure,
So with fair wonders he mine eyes betrayeth
  That my wounds, and his wrongs, become my
    pleasure:
    Till for more spite to Myra's heart he flieth,
    Where, living to the world, to me he dieth.

FULKE GREVILLE, LORD BROOKE

Youth and Maturity

THE nurse-life wheat, within his green husk growing,
    Flatters our hope, and tickles our desire,
Nature's true riches in sweet beauties showing,
    Which set all hearts, with labour's love, on fire.
No less fair is the wheat when golden ear
    Shows unto hope the joys of near enjoying;
Fair and sweet is the bud, more sweet and fair
    The rose, which proves that time is not destroying.
Caelica, your youth, the morning of delight,
    Enamelled o'er with beauties white and red,
All sense and thoughts did to belief invite,
    That love and glory there are brought to bed;
      And your ripe years love none; he goes no higher,
      Turns all the spirits of man into desire.

THOMAS LODGE
[1556?-1625]

All Things Revive Save the Lover

O SHADY vales, O fair enrichèd meads,
  O sacred woods, sweet fields, and rising mountains;
O painted flowers, green herbs where Flora treads,
  Refresh'd by wanton winds and wat'ry fountains!
O all you wingèd choristers of wood,
  That perch'd aloft your former pains report,
And straight again recount with pleasant mood
  Your present joys in sweet and seemly sort!
O all you creatures whosoever thrive
  On mother earth, in seas, by air, by fire!—
More blest are you than I here under sun:
Love dies in me, whenas he doth revive
  In you: I perish under beauty's ire,
Where after storms, winds, frosts, your life is won.

28

ROBERT GREENE
[1560-1592]

Ah! were she pitiful as she is fair,
　Or but as mild as she is seeming so,
Then were my hopes greater than my despair,
　Then all the world were heaven, nothing woe.
Ah! were her heart relenting as her hand,
　That seems to melt even with the mildest touch,
Then knew I where to seat me in a land
　Under wide heavens, but yet there is none such.
So as she shows she seems the budding rose,
　Yet sweeter far than is an earthly flower;
Sov'ran of beauty, like the spray she grows;
　Compass'd she is with thorns and canker'd bower.
　　Yet were she willing to be pluck'd and worn,
　　She would be gather'd, though she grew on
　　　thorn.

HENRY CONSTABLE
[1562-1613]

To Sir Philip Sidney's Soul

GIVE pardon, blessèd soul, to my bold cries,
  If they (importune) interrupt thy song
  Which now, with joyful notes, thou sing'st among
The angel-choristers of heavenly skies;
Give pardon eke, sweet soul, to my slow cries,
  That since I saw thee now it is so long,
  And yet the tears that unto thee belong
To thee as yet they did not sacrifice.
I did not know that thou wert dead before,
  I did not feel the grief I did sustain:
The greater stroke astonisheth the more,
  Astonishment takes from us sense of pain.
    I stood amazed when others' tears begun,
    And now begin to weep when they have done.

SAMUEL DANIEL
[1562-1619]

Delia

FAIR is my Love, and cruel as she's fair;
  Her brow shades frowns, although her eyes are
    sunny,
Her smiles are lightning, though her pride despair,
  And her disdains are gall, her favours honey:
A modest maid, deck'd with a blush of honour,
  Whose feet do tread green paths of youth and love;
The wonder of all eyes that look upon her,
  Sacred on earth, design'd a Saint above.
Chastity and beauty, which were deadly foes,
  Live reconcilèd friends within her brow;
And had she pity to conjoin with those,
  Then who had heard the plaints I utter now?
    For had she not been fair, and thus unkind,
    My Muse had slept, and none had known my
      mind.

SAMUEL DANIEL

The Moth

I

My spotless love hovers with purest wings,
    About the temple of the proudest frame,
Where blaze those lights, fairest of earthly things,
    Which clear our clouded world with brightest
    flame.
My ambitious thoughts, confinèd in her face;
    Affect no honour but what She can give;
My hopes do rest in limits of her grace;
    I weigh no comfort unless she relieve.
For She, that can my heart unparadise,
    Holds in her fairest hand what dearest is,
My Fortune's wheel's the circle of her eyes,
    Whose rolling grace deign once a turn of bliss.
      All my life's sweet consists in her alone;
      So much I love the most Unloving one.

SAMUEL DANIEL

AND yet I cannot reprehend the flight
   Or blame th' attempt presuming so to soar;
The mounting venture for a high delight
   Did make the honour of the fall the more.
For who gets wealth, that puts not from the shore?
   Danger hath honour, great designs their fame;
Glory doth follow, courage goes before;
   And though th' event oft answers not the same,
Suffice that high attempts have never shame.
   The mean observer, whom base safety keeps,
Lives without honour, dies without a name,
   And in eternal darkness ever sleeps:
     And therefore, *Delia*, 'tis to me no blot
     To have attempted, tho' attain'd thee not.

SAMUEL DANIEL

Beauty's Lease

BEAUTY, sweet Love, is like the morning dew,
　Whose short refresh upon the tender green
Cheers for a time, but till the sun doth show;
　And straight 'tis gone as it had never been.
Soon doth it fade that makes the fairest flourish,
　Short is the glory of the blushing rose;
The hue which thou so carefully dost nourish,
　Yet which at length thou must be forced to lose,
When thou, surcharged with burthen of thy years,
　Shalt bend thy wrinkles homeward to the earth;
And that, in Beauty's Lease expired, appears
　　The Date of Age, the Calends of our Death—
　　　But ah, no more!—this must not be foretold,
　　　For women grieve to think they must be old.

SAMUEL DANIEL

Quand Vous Serez Bien Vieille

WHEN men shall find thy flower, thy glory, pass,
    And thou with careful brow sitting alone
Received hast this message from thy glass,
    That tells the truth and says that all is gone,
Fresh shalt thou see in me the wounds thou madest,
    Though spent thy flame, in me the heat remaining:
I that have loved thee thus before thou fadest,
    My faith shall wax, when thou art in thy waning.
The world shall find this miracle in me,
    That fire can burn when all the matter's spent;
Then what my faith hath been thyself shalt see,
    And that thou wast unkind thou mayst repent—
        Thou mayst repent that thou hast scorned my
        tears,
        When winter snows upon thy sable hairs.

SAMUEL DANIEL

Prayer to Sleep

CARE-CHARMER Sleep, son of the sable Night,
    Brother to Death, in silent darkness born,
Relieve my languish and restore the light;
    With dark forgetting of my care, return:
And let the day be time enough to mourn
    The shipwreck of my ill-adventured youth:
Let waking eyes suffice to wail their scorn,
    Without the torment of the night's untruth.
Cease dreams, the images of day's desires,
    To model forth the passions of the morrow;
Never let rising Sun approve you liars,
    To add more grief to aggravate my sorrow.
      Still let me sleep, embracing clouds in vain,
      And never wake to feel the day's disdain.

SAMUEL DANIEL

The Trophies

LET others sing of Knights and Paladines,
  In aged accents and untimely words,
Paint shadows in imaginary lines,
  Which well the reach of their high wit records.
But I must sing of thee, and those fair eyes
  Authentic shall my verse in time to come,
When yet th' unborn shall say, Lo, where she lies!
  Whose beauty made him speak, that else was
    dumb!
These are the arcs, the trophies I erect,
  That fortify thy name against old age;
And these thy sacred virtues must protect
  Against the Dark, and Time's consuming rage.
    Though th' error of my youth in them appear,
    Suffice, they show I lived, and loved thee dear.

MARK ALEXANDER BOYD
[1563-1601]

Sonet

FRA bank to bank, fra wood to wood I rin,
   Ourhailit with my feeble fantasie;
   Like til a leaf that fallis from a tree,
Or til a reed ourblawin with the win.

Twa gods guides me: the ane of tham is blin,
   Yea and a bairn brocht up in vanitie;
   The next a wife ingenrit of the sea,
And lichter nor a dauphin with her fin.

Unhappy is the man for evermair
That tills the sand and sawis in the air;
   But twice unhappier is he, I lairn,
That feidis in his hairt a mad desire,
And follows on a woman throw the fire,
   Led by a blind and teachit by a bairn.

CHARLES BEST
[*d.* 1602]

The Moon

LOOK how the pale queen of the silent night
   Doth cause the Ocean to attend upon her,
And he, as long as she is in his sight,
   With his full tide is ready her to honour;
But when the silver waggon of the Moon
   Is mounted up so high he cannot follow,
The sea calls home his crystal waves to moan,
   And with low ebb doth manifest his sorrow.
So you, that are the sovereign of my heart,
   Have all my joys attending on your will,
My joys low-ebbing when you do depart—
   When you return, their tide my heart doth fill:
     So as you come, and as you do depart,
     Joys ebb and flow within my tender heart.

JOSHUA SYLVESTER
[1563-1618]

Amor Ineluctabilis

WERE I as base as is the lowly plain,
  And you, my Love, as high as heaven above,
Yet should the thoughts of me, your humble swain,
  Ascend to heaven in honour of my Love.
Were I as high as heaven above the plain,
  And you, my Love, as humble and as low
As are the deepest bottoms of the main,
  Wheresoe'er you were, with you my love should go.
Were you the earth, dear Love, and I the skies,
  My love should shine on you like to the Sun,
And look upon you with ten thousand eyes
    Till heaven waxed blind, and till the world were
      done.
    Wheresoe'er I am—below or else above you—
    Wheresoe'er you are, my heart shall truly love
      you.

MICHAEL DRAYTON
[1563-1631]

A Play with Proverbs

As Love and I, late harbour'd in one Inn,
  With proverbs thus each other entertain,
In love there is no lack, thus I begin;
  Fair words make fools, replieth he again;
That spares to speak doth spare to speed, quoth I,
  As well, saith he, *too forward as too slow:*
Fortune assists the boldest, I reply;
  A hasty man, quoth he, *ne'er wanted woe.*
Labour is light where love, quoth I, *doth pay;*
  Saith he, *Light burden's heavy, if far borne:*
Quoth I, *The main lost, throw the bye away;*
  You have spun a fair thread, he replies in scorn.
    And having thus awhile each other thwarted,
    Fools as we met, so fools again we parted.

MICHAEL DRAYTON

Against Knowledge in Loving

WHY should your fair eyes with such sovran grace
　Disperse their rays on every vulgar spirit,
Whilst I in darkness in the self-same place
　Get not one glance to recompense my merit?
So doth the plowman gaze the wand'ring star,
　And only rest contented with the light,
That never learn'd what constellations are
　Beyond the bent of his unknowing sight.
O why should beauty—custom to obey—
　To their gross sense apply herself so ill?
Would 'God I were as ignorant as they,
　When I am made unhappy by my skill;
　　Only compell'd on this poor good to boast—
　　Heavens are not kind to them that know them
　　most!

MICHAEL DRAYTON

Her Fame

How many paltry, foolish, painted things,
   That now in coaches trouble every street,
Shall be forgotten, whom no poet sings,
   Ere they be well wrapped in their winding-sheet?
Where I to thee eternity shall give,
   When nothing else remaineth of these days,
And Queens hereafter shall be glad to live
   Upon the alms of thy superfluous praise.
Virgins and matrons, reading these my rhymes,
   Shall be so much delighted with thy story,
That they shall grieve they lived not in these times,
   To have seen thee, their sex's only glory.
    So shalt thou fly above the vulgar throng,
    Still to survive in my immortal song.

MICHAEL DRAYTON

The Guest

Love, banished heaven, in earth was held in scorn,
  Wandering abroad in need and beggary,
And wanting friends, though of a goddess born,
  Yet craved the alms of such as passèd by;
I, like a man devout and charitable,
  Clothèd the naked, lodged this wandering guest,
With sighs and tears still furnishing his table,
  With what might make the miserable blest.
But this ungrateful, for my good desert,
  Inticed my thoughts against me to conspire,
Who gave consent to steal away my heart,
  And set my breast, his lodging, on a fire.
    Well, well, my friends, when beggars grow thus
      bold,
    No marvel then though charity grow cold!

MICHAEL DRAYTON

Farewell

SINCE there's no help, come let us kiss and part,—
  Nay I have done, you get no more of me;
And I am glad, yea, glad with all my heart,
  That thus so cleanly I myself can free;
Shake hands for ever, cancel all our vows,
  And when we meet at any time again,
Be it not seen in either of our brows
  That we one jot of former love retain.
Now at the last gasp of Love's latest breath,
  When, his pulse failing, Passion speechless lies,
When Faith is kneeling by his bed of death,
  And Innocence is closing up his eyes,—
    Now if thou wouldst, when all have given him
      over,
    From death to life thou mightst him yet recover!

IGNOTUS

(From *Musica Transalpina*. 1597)

ZEPHYRUS brings the time that sweetly scenteth
  With flowers and herbs which winter's frost exileth;
Progne now chirpeth, Philomel lamenteth,
  Flora the garlands white and red compileth;
Fields do rejoice, the frowning sky relenteth,
  Jove to behold his dearest daughter smileth;
The air, the water, the earth to joy consenteth,
  Each creature now to love him reconcileth.
But with me, wretch, the storms of woe perséver,
  And heavy sighs which from my heart she straineth,
That took the key thereof to heaven for ever;
  So that singing of birds and springtime's flow'ring,
And ladies' love that men's affection gaineth,
  Are like a desert and cruel beasts devouring.

WILLIAM SHAKESPEARE
[1564-1616]

Twenty-seven Sonnets

I

WHEN I do count the clock that tells the time,
  And see the brave day sunk in hideous night;
When I behold the violet past prime,
  And sable curls all silver'd o'er with white;
When lofty trees I see barren of leaves
  Which erst from heat did canopy the herd,
And summer's green all girded up in sheaves
  Borne on the bier with white and bristly beard,
Then of thy beauty do I question make,
  That thou among the wastes of time must go,
Since sweets and beauties do themselves forsake,
  And die as fast as they see others grow;
    And nothing 'gainst Time's scythe can make
    defence
    Save breed, to brave him when he takes thee
    hence.

WILLIAM SHAKESPEARE

11

SHALL I compare thee to a summer's day?
  Thou art more lovely and more temperate:
Rough winds do shake the darling buds of May,
  And summer's lease hath all too short a date;
Sometime too hot the eye of heaven shines,
  And often is his gold complexion dimm'd;
And every fair from fair sometime declines,
  By chance or nature's changing course untrimm'd;
But thy eternal summer shall not fade
  Nor lose possession of that fair thou owest:
Nor shall Death brag thou wander'st in his shade,
  When in eternal lines to time thou growest;
    So long as men can breathe or eyes can see,
    So long lives this and this gives life to thee.

WILLIAM SHAKESPEARE

WHEN, in disgrace with fortune and men's eyes,
    I all alone beweep my outcast state,
And trouble deaf heaven with my bootless cries,
    And look upon myself and curse my fate,
Wishing me like to one more rich in hope,
    Featured like him, like him with friends possess'd,
Desiring this man's art and that man's scope,
    With what I most enjoy contented least;
Yet in these thoughts myself almost despising,
    Haply I think on thee, and then my state,
Like to the lark at break of day arising
    From sullen earth, sings hymns at heaven's gate;
      For thy sweet love remember'd such wealth
        brings
      That then I scorn to change my state with kings.

WILLIAM SHAKESPEARE

WHEN to the sessions of sweet silent thought
  I summon up remembrance of things past,
I sigh the lack of many a thing I sought,
  And with old woes new wail my dear time's waste;
Then can I drown an eye, unused to flow,
  For precious friends hid in death's dateless night,
And weep afresh love's long since cancell'd woe,
  And moan the expense of many a vanish'd sight:
Then can I grieve at grievances foregone,
  And heavily from woe to woe tell o'er
The sad account of fore-bemoanèd moan,
  Which I now pay as if not paid before.
    But if the while I think on thee, dear friend,
    All losses are restored and sorrows end.

WILLIAM SHAKESPEARE

V

THY bosom is endeared with all hearts,
  Which I by lacking have supposed dead,
And there reigns love and all love's loving parts,
  And all those friends which I thought buried.
How many a holy and obsequious tear
  Hath dear religious love stol'n from mine eye
As interest of the dead, which now appear
  But things removed that hidden in thee lie!
Thou art the grave where buried love doth live,
  Hung with the trophies of my lovers gone,
Who all their parts of me to thee did give;
  That due of many now is thine alone:
    Their images I loved I view in thee,
    And thou, all they, hast all the all of me.

WILLIAM SHAKESPEARE

VI

IF thou survive my well-contented day,
  When that churl Death my bones with dust shall
    cover,
And shalt by fortune once more re-survey
  These poor rude lines of thy deceased lover,
Compare them with the bettering of the time,
  And though they be outstripp'd by every pen,
Reserve them for my love, not for their rhyme,
  Exceeded by the height of happier men.
O, then vouchsafe me but this loving thought:
  "Had my friend's Muse grown with this growing
    age,
A dearer birth than this his love had brought,
  To march in ranks of better equipage;
    But since he died and poets better prove,
    Theirs for their style I'll read, his for his love."

WILLIAM SHAKESPEARE

FULL many a glorious morning have I seen
 Flatter the mountain-tops with sovereign eye,
Kissing with golden face the meadows green,
 Gilding pale streams with heavenly alchemy;
Anon permit the basest clouds to ride
 With ugly rack on his celestial face,
And from the forlorn world his visage hide,
 Stealing unseen to west with this disgrace:
Even so my sun one early morn did shine
 With all-triumphant splendour on my brow;
But out, alack! he was but one hour mine;
 The region cloud had mask'd him from me now.
 Yet him for this my love no whit disdaineth;
 Suns of the world may stain when heaven's sun
 staineth.

WILLIAM SHAKESPEARE

VIII

BEING your slave, what should I do but tend
　Upon the hours and times of your desire?
I have no precious time at all to spend,
　Nor services to do, till you require.
Nor dare I chide the world-without-end hour
　Whilst I, my sovereign, watch the clock for you,
Nor think the bitterness of absence sour
　When you have bid your servant once adieu;
Nor dare I question with my jealous thought
　Where you may be, or your affairs suppose,
But, like a sad slave, stay and think of nought
　Save, where you are how happy you make those.
　　So true a fool is love that in your Will,
　　Though you do any thing, he thinks no ill.

WILLIAM SHAKESPEARE

LIKE as the waves make towards the pebbled shore,
    So do our minutes hasten to their end;
Each changing place with that which goes before,
    In sequent toil all forwards do contend.
Nativity, once in the main of light,
    Crawls to maturity, wherewith being crown'd,
Crooked eclipses 'gainst his glory fight,
    And Time that gave doth now his gift confound.
Time doth transfix the flourish set on youth
    And delves the parallels in beauty's brow,
Feeds on the rarities of Nature's truth,
    And nothing stands but for his scythe to mow;
        And yet to times in hope my verse shall stand,
        Praising thy worth, despite his cruel hand.

WILLIAM SHAKESPEARE

X

WHEN I have seen by Time's fell hand defaced
  The rich proud cost of outworn buried age;
When sometime lofty towers I see down-razed,
  And brass eternal slave to mortal rage:
When I have seen the hungry ocean gain
  Advantage on the kingdom of the shore,
And the firm soil win of the watery main,
  Increasing store with loss and loss with store;
When I have seen such interchange of state,
  Or state itself confounded to decay;
Ruin hath taught me thus to ruminate,
  That time will come and take my love away.
    This thought is as a death, which cannot choose
    But weep to have that which it fears to lose.

WILLIAM SHAKESPEARE

SINCE brass, nor stone, nor earth, nor boundless sea,
　　But sad mortality o'er-sways their power,
How with this rage shall beauty hold a plea,
　　Whose action is no stronger than a flower?
O, how shall summer's honey breath hold out
　　Against the wreckful siege of battering days,
When rocks impregnable are not so stout,
　　Nor gates of steel so strong, but time decays?
O fearful meditation! where, alack,
　　Shall Time's best jewel from Time's quest lie hid?
Or what strong hand can hold his swift foot back?
　　Or who his spoil of beauty can forbid?
　　　　O, none, unless this miracle have might,
　　　　That in black ink my love may still shine bright.

XII

No longer mourn for me when I am dead,
  Than you shall hear the surly sullen bell
Give warning to the world that I am fled
  From this vile world, with vilest worms to dwell:
Nay, if you read this line, remember not
  The hand that writ it; for I love you so
That I in your sweet thoughts would be forgot,
  If thinking on me then should make you woe.
O, if, I say, you look upon this verse,
  When I perhaps compounded am with clay,
Do not so much as my poor name rehearse,
  But let your love even with my life decay,
    Lest the wise world should look into your moan,
    And mock you with me after I am gone.

WILLIAM SHAKESPEARE

THAT time of year thou mayst in me behold
   When yellow leaves, or none, or few, do hang
Upon those boughs which shake against the cold,
   Bare ruin'd choirs, where late the sweet birds sang.
In me thou see'st the twilight of such day
   As after sunset fadeth in the west,
Which by and by black night doth take away,
   Death's second self, that seals up all in rest.
In me thou see'st the glowing of such fire
   That on the ashes of his youth doth lie,
As the death-bed whereon it must expire,
   Consumed with that which it was nourish'd by.
     This thou perceivest, which makes thy love more
      strong,
     To love that well which thou must leave ere long.

WILLIAM SHAKESPEARE

X I V

FAREWELL! thou art too dear for my possessing,
  And like enough thou know'st thy estimate:
The charter of thy worth gives thee releasing;
  My bonds in thee are all determinate.
For how do I hold thee but by thy granting?
  And for that riches where is my deserving?
The cause of this fair gift in me is wanting,
  And so my patent back again is swerving.
Thyself thou gavest, thy own worth then not knowing,
  Or me, to whom thou gavest it, else mistaking;
So thy great gift, upon misprision growing,
  Comes home again, on better judgment making.
    Thus have I had thee as a dream doth flatter,
    In sleep a king, but waking no such matter.

WILLIAM SHAKESPEARE

X V

THEN hate me when thou wilt; if ever, now;
   Now, while the world is bent my deeds to cross,
Join with the spite of fortune, make me bow,
   And do not drop in for an after-loss:
Ah, do not, when my heart hath 'scaped this sorrow,
   Come in the rearward of a conquer'd woe:
Give not a windy night a rainy morrow,
   To linger out a purposed overthrow.
If thou wilt leave me, do not leave me last,
   When other petty griefs have done their spite,
But in the onset come; so shall I taste
   At first the very worst of fortune's might,
     And other strains of woe, which now seem woe,
     Compared with loss of thee will not seem so.

WILLIAM SHAKESPEARE

X V I

THEY that have power to hurt and will do none,
   That do not do the thing they most do show,
Who, moving others, are themselves as stone,
   Unmovèd, cold, and to temptation slow,
They rightly do inherit heaven's graces
   And husband Nature's riches from expense:
They are the lords and owners of their faces,
   Others but stewards of their excellence.
The summer's flower is to the summer sweet,
   Though to itself it only live and die,
But if that flower with base infection meet,
   The basest weed outbraves his dignity:
     For sweetest things turn sourest by their deeds;
     Lilies that fester smell far worse than weeds.

WILLIAM SHAKESPEARE

How like a winter hath my absence been
From thee, the pleasure of the fleeting year!
What freezings have I felt, what dark days seen!
What old December's bareness every where!
And yet this time removed was summer's time,
The teeming autumn, big with rich increase,
Bearing the wanton burden of the prime,
Like widow'd wombs after their lords' decease:
Yet this abundant issue seem'd to me
But hope of orphans and unfather'd fruit;
For summer and his pleasures wait on thee,
And, thou away, the very birds are mute;
Or, if they sing, 'tis with so dull a cheer
That leaves look pale, dreading the winter's
near.

WILLIAM SHAKESPEARE

From you have I been absent in the spring,
  When proud-pied April, dress'd in all his trim,
Hath put a spirit of youth in every thing,
  That heavy Saturn laugh'd and leap'd with him.
Yet nor the lays of birds nor the sweet smell
  Of different flowers in odour and in hue
Could make me any summer's story tell,
  Or from their proud lap pluck them where they
      grew;
Nor did I wonder at the lily's white,
  Nor praise the deep vermilion in the rose;
They were but sweet, but figures of delight,
  Drawn after you, you pattern of all those.
    Yet seem'd it winter still, and, you away,
    As with your shadow I with these did play.

WILLIAM SHAKESPEARE

THE froward violet thus did I chide:
  Sweet thief, whence didst thou steal thy sweet
    that smells,
If not from my Love's breath? The purple pride
  Which on thy soft cheek for complexion dwells
In my Love's veins thou hast too grossly dyed.
The lily I condemnèd for thy hand,
  And buds of marjoram had stol'n thy hair:
The roses fearfully on thorns did stand,
  One blushing shame, another white despair;
A third, nor red nor white, had stol'n of both,
  And to his robbery had annex'd thy breath;
But, for his theft, in pride of all his growth
  A vengeful canker eat him up to death.
    More flowers I noted, yet I none could see
    But sweet or colour it had stol'n from thee.

WILLIAM SHAKESPEARE

x x

My love is strengthen'd, though more weak in
 seeming;
 I love not less, though less the show appear:
That love is merchandised whose rich esteeming
 The owner's tongue doth publish every where.
Our love was new and then but in the spring,
 When I was wont to greet it with my lays,
As Philomel in summer's front doth sing
 And stops her pipe in growth of riper days:
Not that the summer is less pleasant now
 Than when her mournful hymns did hush the
 night,
But that wild music burthens every bough
 And sweets grown common lose their dear delight.
 Therefore like her I sometime hold my tongue,
 Because I would not dull you with my song.

WILLIAM SHAKESPEARE

X X I

To me, fair friend, you never can be old,
  For as you were when first your eye I eyed,
Such seems your beauty still. Three winters cold
  Have from the forests shook three summers' pride,
Three beauteous springs to yellow autumn turn'd
  In process of the seasons have I seen,
Three April perfumes in three hot Junes burn'd,
  Since first I saw you fresh, which yet are green.
Ah! yet doth beauty, like a dial-hand,
  Steal from his figure and no pace perceived;
So your sweet hue, which methinks still doth stand,
  Hath motion and mine eye may be deceived:
    For fear of which, hear this, thou age unbred:
    Ere you were born was beauty's summer dead.

WILLIAM SHAKESPEARE

XXII

When in the chronicle of wasted time
  I see descriptions of the fairest wights,
And beauty making beautiful old rhyme
  In praise of ladies dead and lovely knights,
Then, in the blazon of sweet beauty's best,
  Of hand, of foot, of lip, of eye, of brow,
I see their antique pen would have express'd
  Even such a beauty as your master now.
So all their praises are but prophecies
  Of this our time, all you prefiguring;
And, for they look'd but with divining eyes,
  They had not skill enough your worth to sing:
    For we, which now behold these present days,
    Have eyes to wonder, but lack tongues to praise.

WILLIAM SHAKESPEARE

XXIII

NOT mine own fears, nor the prophetic soul
   Of the wide world dreaming on things to come,
Can yet the lease of my true love control,
   Supposed as forfeit to a confined doom.
The mortal moon hath her eclipse endured
   And the sad augurs mock their own presage;
Incertainties now crown themselves assured,
   And peace proclaims olives of endless age.
Now with the drops of this most balmy time
   My love looks fresh, and Death to me subscribes
Since, spite of him, I'll live in this poor rhyme,
   While he insults o'er dull and speechless tribes:
     And thou in this shalt find thy monument,
     When tyrants' crests and tombs of brass are
      spent.

WILLIAM SHAKESPEARE

XXIV

O, NEVER say that I was false of heart,
  Though absence seem'd my flame to qualify!
As easy might I from myself depart
  As from my soul, which in thy breast doth lie:
That is my home of love: if I have ranged,
  Like him that travels I return again,
Just to the time, not with the time exchanged,
  So that myself bring water for my stain.
Never believe, though in my nature reign'd
  All frailties that besiege all kinds of blood,
That it could so preposterously be stain'd,
    To leave for nothing all thy sum of good;
      For nothing this wide universe I call,
      Save thou, my rose; in it thou art my all.

WILLIAM SHAKESPEARE

X X V

LET me not to the marriage of true minds
 Admit impediments. Love is not love
Which alters when it alteration finds,
 Or bends with the remover to remove:
O, no! it is an ever-fixèd mark
 That looks on tempests and is never shaken:
It is the star to every wandering bark,
 Whose worth's unknown, although his height be
  taken.
Love's not Time's fool, though rosy lips and cheeks
 Within his bending sickle's compass come;
Love alters not with his brief hours and weeks,
 But bears it out even to the edge of doom.
  If this be error and upon me proved,
  I never writ, nor no man ever loved.

WILLIAM SHAKESPEARE

X X V I

THE expense of spirit in a waste of shame
  Is lust in action; and till action, lust
Is perjured, murderous, bloody, full of blame,
  Savage, extreme, rude, cruel, not to trust,
Enjoy'd no sooner but despisèd straight,
  Past reason hunted, and no sooner had
Past reason hated, as a swallow'd bait
  On purpose laid to make the taker mad;
Mad in pursuit and in possession so;
  Had, having, and in quest to have, extreme;
A bliss in proof, and proved, a very woe;
  Before, a joy proposed; behind, a dream.
    All this the world well knows; yet none knows
      well
    To shun the heaven that leads men to this hell.

WILLIAM SHAKESPEARE

Poor soul, the centre of my sinful earth,
　Feeding these rebel powers that thee array,
Why dost thou pine within and suffer dearth,
　Painting thy outward walls so costly gay?
Why so large cost, having so short a lease,
　Dost thou upon thy fading mansion spend?
Shall worms, inheritors of this excess,
　Eat up thy charge? is this thy body's end?
Then, soul, live thou upon thy servant's loss,
　And let that pine to aggravate thy store:
Buy terms divine in selling hours of dross;
　Within be fed, without be rich no more:
　　So shalt thou feed on Death, that feeds on men,
　　And Death once dead, there's no more dying
　　then.

THOMAS CAMPION
[1567-1620]

Spells

THRICE toss these oaken ashes in the air,
　　And thrice three times tie up this true-love's-knot;
Thrice sit thee down in this enchanted chair,
　　And murmur soft, "She will, or she will not."
Go burn these poisoned weeds in that blue fire—
　　This cypress gathered at a dead man's grave,
These screech-owl's feathers, and this pricking briar,
　　That all thy thorny cares an end may have.
Then come, you fairies, dance with me a round,
　　Dance in this circle, let my Love be centre,
Melodiously breathe out a charming sound,
　　Melt her hard heart, that some remorse may enter.
　　　In vain are all the charms I can devise!
　　　She hath an art to break them with her eyes.

BARNABE BARNES
[1569-1609]

Content

Ah, sweet Content! where is thy mild abode?
  Is it with shepherds and light-hearted swains
Which sing upon the downs and pipe abroad,
  Tending their flocks and cattle on the plains?
Ah, sweet Content! where dost thou safely rest?
  In heaven, with angels which the praises sing
Of Him that made, and rules at his behest,
  The minds and hearts of every living thing?
Ah, sweet Content! where doth thine harbour hold?
  Is it in churches with religious men
Which please the gods with prayers manifold,
  And in their studies meditate it then?—
    Whether thou dost in heaven or earth appear,
    Be where thou wilt, thou will not harbour here.

SIR JOHN DAVIES
[1570-1626]

Visitors

WHILES in my Soul I feel the soft warm hand
   Of Grace, to thaw the frozen dregs of sin,
She, angel, armed, on Eden's walls doth stand,
   To keep out outward joys that would come in.
But when that holy hand is ta'en away,
   And that my Soul congealeth as before,
She outward comforts seeks with care each way,
   And runs to meet them at each sense's door.
Yet they but at the first sight only please,
   Then shrink, or breed abhorred satiety;
But divine comforts, far unlike to these,
   Do please the more, the more they stay and be.
   Then outward joys I inwardly detest,
     Sith they stay not, or stay but in unrest.

JOHN DONNE
[1573-1631]

Death

DEATH, be not proud, though some have callèd thee
   Mighty and dreadful, for thou art not so;
   For those whom thou think'st thou dost overthrow
Die not, poor Death; nor yet canst thou kill me.
From rest and sleep, which but thy pictures be,
   Much pleasure: then from thee much more must
      flow;
   And soonest our best men with thee do go—
Rest of their bones and souls' delivery!
Thou'rt slave to fate, chance, kings and desperate
      men,
   And dost with poison, war, and sickness dwell;
   And poppy or charms can make us sleep as well,
And better than thy stroke. Why swell'st thou then?
    One short sleep past, we wake eternally,
    And death shall be no more: Death, thou shalt
    die.

RICHARD BARNFIELD
[1574-1627]

To his Friend Maister R. L. in Praise of Music and Poetry

IF music and sweet poetry agree,
  As they must needs, the sister and the brother,
Then must the love be great 'twixt thee and me,
  Because thou lov'st the one, and I the other.
Dowland to thee is dear, whose heavenly touch
  Upon the lute doth ravish human sense;
Spenser to me, whose deep conceit is such
  As passing all conceit needs no defence.
Thou lov'st to hear the sweet melodious sound
  That Phœbus' lute, the queen of music, makes;
And I in deep delight am chiefly drowned
  Whenas himself to singing he betakes.
    One god is god of both, as poets feign;
    One knight loves both, and both in thee remain.

WILLIAM ALEXANDER
EARL OF STIRLING [1580-1640]

Two in One

Oh, if thou knew'st how thou thyself dost harm,
   And dost prejudge thy bliss, and spoil my rest;
   Then thou wouldst melt the ice out of thy breast,
And thy relenting heart would kindly warm:
Oh, if thy pride did not our joys controul,
   What world of loving wonders shouldst thou see!
   For if I saw thee once transformed in me,
Then in thy bosom I would pour my soul,
Then all thy thoughts should in my visage shine;
   And if that ought mischanced, thou shouldst not
     moan
   Nor bear the burthen of thy griefs alone.
No, I would have my share in what were thine:
   And whilst we thus should make our sorrows one,
   This happy harmony would make them none.

WILLIAM DRUMMOND
OF HAWTHORNDEN [1585-1649]

To Sleep

SLEEP, Silence' child, sweet father of soft rest,
  Prince, whose approach peace to all mortal brings,
  Indifferent host to shepherds and to kings,
Sole comforter of minds with grief opprest;
  Lo! by thy charming-rod all breathing things
Lie slumbering, with forgetfulness possest,
  And yet o'er me to spread thy drowsy wings
Thou spares, alas! who cannot be thy guest.
Since I am thine, oh come! but with that face
  To inward light which thou art wont to show;
  With feignèd solace ease a true-felt woe;
Or if, deaf god, thou do deny that grace,
    Come as thou wilt, and that thou wilt bequeath,—
    I long to kiss the image of my death.

WILLIAM DRUMMOND

Primitiæ

ALEXIS, here she stayed; among these pines,
  Sweet hermitress, she did alone repair;
  Here did she spread the treasure of her hair,
More rich than that brought from the Colchian
    mines:
She set her by these muskèd eglantines—
  The happy place the print seems yet to bear;
Her voice did sweeten here thy sugared lines,
  To which winds, trees, beasts, birds, did lend their
    ear;
Me here she first perceived, and here a morn
  Of bright carnations did o'erspread her face;
Here did she sigh, here first my hopes were born,
  And I first got a pledge of promised grace;
    But ah! what served it to be happy so,
    Sith passèd pleasures double but new woe?

WILLIAM DRUMMOND

Spring, Wanting Her

SWEET Spring, thou turn'st with all thy goodly train,
  Thy head with flames, thy mantle bright with
    flowers;
The zephyrs curl the green locks of the plain,
  The clouds for joy in pearls weep down their
    showers:
  Thou turn'st, sweet youth; but ah! my pleasant
    hours
And happy days with thee come not again:
The sad memorials only of my pain
  Do with thee turn, which turn my sweets in sours.
Thou art the same which still thou wast before,
  Delicious, wanton, amiable, fair;
  But she, whose breath embalmed thy wholesome
    air,
Is gone; nor gold nor gems her can restore.
    Neglected Virtue! Seasons go and come,
    While thine, forgot, lie closèd in a tomb.

WILLIAM DRUMMOND

The Book of the World

OF this fair volume which we World do name,
  If we the sheets and leaves could turn with care,
Of Him who it corrects and did it frame,
  We clear might read the art and wisdom rare:
Find out His power which wildest powers doth tame,
  His providence extending everywhere,
  His justice which proud rebels doth not spare,
In every page, no period of the same.
But silly we, like foolish children, rest
  Well pleased with coloured vellum, leaves of gold,
Fair dangling ribbons, leaving what is best,
  On the great writer's sense ne'er taking hold;
    Or if by chance we stay our minds on aught,
    It is some picture on the margin wrought.

WILLIAM DRUMMOND

Content and Resolute

As when it happeneth that some lovely town
  Unto a barbarous besieger falls,
  Who there by sword and flame himself installs,
And, cruel, it in tears and blood doth drown;
  Her beauty spoiled, her citizens made thralls,
His spite yet so can not her all throw down
But that some statue, arch, fane of renown
  Yet lurks unmaimed within her weeping walls:
So, after all the spoil, disgrace, and wrack,
  That time, the world, and death, could bring
    combined,
Amidst that mass of ruins they did make,
  Safe and all scarless yet remains my mind.
    From this so high transcending rapture springs,
    That I, all else defaced, not envy kings.

WILLIAM DRUMMOND

Saint John Baptist

THE last and greatest herald of heaven's King,
  Girt with rough skins, hies to the deserts wild,
Among that savage brood the woods forth bring,
  Which he than man more harmless found and mild.
His food was locusts, and what there doth spring,
  With honey that from virgin hives distilled;
Parcht body, hollow eyes, some uncouth thing
  Made him appear, long since from earth exiled.
There burst he forth: All ye whose hopes rely
  On God, with me amidst these deserts mourn,
  Repent, repent, and from old errors turn!—
Who listened to his voice, obeyed his cry?
    Only the echoes, which he made relent,
    Rung from their flinty caves, Repent! Repent!

WILLIAM BROWNE OF TAVISTOCK
[1590-1645]

The Rose

A ROSE, as fair as ever saw the north,
   Grew in a little garden all alone:
A sweeter flower did Nature ne'er put forth,
   Nor fairer garden yet was never known.
The maidens danced about it morn and noon,
   And learnèd bards of it their ditties made;
The nimble fairies, by the pale-faced moon,
   Watered the root, and kissed her pretty shade.
But, welladay! the gardener careless grew,
   The maids and fairies both were kept away,
And in a drought the caterpillars threw
   Themselves upon the bud and every spray.
     God shield the stock! If heaven send no supplies,
     The fairest blossom of the garden dies.

GEORGE HERBERT
[1593-1632]

Sin

LORD, with what care hast Thou begirt us round!
    Parents first season us; then schoolmasters
Deliver us to laws; they send us bound
    To rules of reason, holy messengers,
Pulpits and Sundays, sorrow dogging sin,
    Afflictions sorted, anguish of all sizes,
Fine nets and stratagems to catch us in,
    Bibles laid open, millions of surprises;
Blessings beforehand, ties of gratefulness,
    The sound of glory ringing in our ears;
Without, our shame; within, our consciences;
    Angels and grace, eternal hopes and fears.
      Yet all these fences and their whole array
      One cunning bosom-sin blows quite away.

WILLIAM HABINGTON
[1605-1645]

Love's Anniversary to the Sun

THOU art returned, great light, to that blest hour
In which I first by marriage, sacred power,
   Joined with Castara hearts: and as the same
   Thy lustre is, as then, so is our flame;
Which had increased, but that by love's decree
'Twas such at first it ne'er could greater be.
   But tell me, glorious lamp, in thy survey
   Of things below thee, what did not decay
By age to weakness?—I since that have seen
The rose bud forth and fade, the tree grow green
   And wither, and the beauty of the field
   With winter wrinkled. Even thyself dost yield
     Something to time, and to thy grave fall
     nigher;—
   But virtuous love is one sweet endless fire.

JOHN MILTON
[1608-1674]

To the Nightingale

O NIGHTINGALE! that on yon bloomy spray
  Warblest at eve, when all the woods are still,
  Thou with fresh hope the lover's heart dost fill,
While the jolly hours lead on propitious May.
Thy liquid notes that close the eye of day,
  First heard before the shallow cuckoo's bill,
  Portend success in love. O, if Jove's will
Have linked that amorous power to thy soft lay,
Now timely sing, ere the rude bird of hate
  Foretell my hopeless doom, in some grove nigh;
As thou from year to year hast sung too late
  For my relief, yet hadst no reason why.
Whether the Muse or Love call thee his mate,
  Both them I serve, and of their train am I.

JOHN MILTON

On His having Arrived at the Age of Twenty-three

How soon hath Time, the subtle thief of youth,
   Stolen on his wing my three-and-twentieth year!
   My hasting days fly on with full career,
But my late spring no bud or blossom shew'th.
Perhaps my semblance might deceive the truth
   That I to manhood am arrived so near;
   And inward ripeness doth much less appear,
That some more timely happy spirits indu'th.
Yet, be it less or more, or soon or slow,
   It shall be still in strictest measure even
     To that same lot, however mean or high,
   Toward which Time leads me, and the will of
     Heaven.
All is, if I have grace to use it so,
   As ever in my great Taskmaster's eye.

JOHN MILTON

When the Assault was Intended to the City

CAPTAIN or Colonel, or Knight in Arms,
  Whose chance on these defenceless doors may seize,
  If deed of honour did thee ever please,
Guard them, and him within protect from harms.
He can requite thee; for he knows the charms
  That call fame on such gentle acts as these,
  And he can spread thy name o'er lands and seas,
Whatever clime the sun's bright circle warms.
Lift not thy spear against the Muses' bower!
  The great Emathian conqueror bid spare
The house of Pindarus, when temple and tower
  Went to the ground; and the repeated air
Of sad Electra's poet had the power
  To save the Athenian walls from ruin bare.

JOHN MILTON

To a Virtuous Young Lady

LADY, that in the prime of earliest youth
   Wisely hast shunned the broad way and the green,
   And with those few art eminently seen
That labour up the hill of heavenly Truth,
The better part with Mary and with Ruth
   Chosen thou hast; and they that overween,
   And at thy growing virtues fret their spleen,
No anger find in thee, but pity and ruth.
Thy care is fixed, and zealously attends
   To fill thy odorous lamp with deeds of light,
     And hope that reaps not shame. Therefore be
     sure
Thou, when the Bridegroom with his feastful friends
   Passes to bliss at the mid-hour of night,
     Hast gained thy entrance, virgin wise and pure.

JOHN MILTON

To the Lady Margaret Ley

DAUGHTER to that good Earl, once President
  Of England's Council and her Treasury,
  Who lived in both unstained with gold or fee,
And left them both, more in himself content,
Till the sad breaking of that Parliament
  Broke him, as that dishonest victory
  At Chæronea, fatal to liberty,
Killed with report that old man eloquent:
Though later born than to have known the days
  Wherein your father flourished, yet by you,
    Madam, methinks I see him living yet:
So well your words his noble virtues praise
  That all both judge you to relate them true
    And to possess them, honoured Margaret.

JOHN MILTON

To Mr. H. Lawes on His Airs

HARRY, whose tuneful and well-measured song
   First taught our English music how to span
   Words with just note and accent, not to scan
With Midas' ears, committing short and long,
Thy worth and skill exempts thee from the throng,
   With praise enough for Envy to look wan;
   To after age thou shalt be writ the man
That with smooth air couldst humour best our
    tongue.
Thou honour'st Verse, and Verse must send her wing
   To honour thee, the priest of Phœbus' quire,
      That tunest their happiest lines in hymn or story.
   Dante shall give Fame leave to set thee higher
Than his Casella, whom he wooed to sing,
      Met in the milder shades of Purgatory.

JOHN MILTON

On the Religious Memory of Mrs. Catherine Thomson, my Christian Friend, deceased Dec. 16, 1646

WHEN Faith and Love, which parted from thee never,
  Had ripened thy just soul to dwell with God,
  Meekly thou didst resign this earthy load
Of death, called life, which us from life doth sever.
Thy works, and alms, and all thy good endeavour,
  Stayed not behind, nor in the grave were trod;
  But, as Faith pointed with her golden rod,
Followed thee up to joy and bliss for ever.
Love led them on; and Faith, who knew them best
  Thy handmaids, clad them o'er with purple
    beams
And azure wings, that up they flew so drest,
  And speak the truth of thee on glorious themes
Before the Judge; who thenceforth bid thee rest,
  And drink thy fill of pure immortal streams.

95

JOHN MILTON

To the Lord General Cromwell, May 1652, on the Proposals of Certain Ministers at the Committee for Propagation of the Gospel

CROMWELL, our chief of men, who through a cloud
    Not of war only, but detractions rude,
    Guided by faith and matchless fortitude,
To peace and truth thy glorious way hast ploughed,
And on the neck of crownèd Fortune proud
    Hast reared God's trophies, and His work pursued,
    While Darwen stream, with blood of Scots imbrued,
And Dunbar field, resounds thy praises loud,
And Worcester's laureate wreath: yet much remains
    To conquer still; Peace hath her victories
    No less renowned than War: new foes arise,
Threatening to bind our souls with secular chains.
    Help us to save free conscience from the paw
    Of hireling wolves, whose Gospel is their maw.

JOHN MILTON

To Sir Henry Vane the Younger

VANE, young in years, but in sage counsel old,
　Than whom a better senator ne'er held
　The helm of Rome, when gowns, not arms,
　　repelled
The fierce Epirot and the African bold,
Whether to settle peace, or to unfold
　The drift of hollow states hard to be spelled;
　Then to advise how war may, best upheld,
Move by her two main nerves, iron and gold,
In all her equipage; besides, to know
　Both spiritual power and civil, what each means,
　　What severs each, thou hast learned, which few
　　　have done.
The bounds of either sword to thee we owe:
　Therefore on thy firm hand Religion leans
　　In peace, and reckons-thee her eldest son.

JOHN MILTON

On the Late Massacre in Piedmont

AVENGE, O Lord, thy slaughtered saints, whose bones
   Lie scattered on the Alpine mountains cold;
   Even them who kept thy truth so pure of old,
When all our Fathers worshipped stocks and stones,
Forget not: in thy book record their groans
   Who were thy sheep, and in their ancient fold
   Slain by the bloody Piedmontese, that rolled
Mother with infant down the rocks. Their moans
The vales redoubled to the hills, and they
   To heaven. Their martyred blood and ashes sow
O'er all the Italian fields, where still doth sway
   The triple Tyrant; that from these may grow
A hundredfold, who, having learnt thy way,
   Early may fly the Babylonian woe.

JOHN MILTON

On His Blindness

WHEN I consider how my light is spent,
  Ere half my days in this dark world and wide,
  And that one talent which is death to hide
Lodged with me useless, though my soul more bent
To serve therewith my Maker, and present
  My true account, lest he, returning, chide,
  "Doth God exact day-labour, light denied?"
I fondly ask. But Patience, to prevent
That murmur, soon replies, "God doth not need
  Either man's work or his own gifts. Who best
    Bear his mild yoke, they serve him best. His
    State
Is kingly. Thousands at his bidding speed,
  And post o'er land and ocean without rest;
    They also serve who only stand and wait."

JOHN MILTON

To Mr. Lawrence

LAWRENCE, of virtuous father virtuous son,
  Now that the fields are dank, and ways are mire,
  Where shall we sometimes meet, and by the fire
Help waste a sullen day, what may be won
From the hard season gaining? Time will run
  On smoother, till Favonius reinspire
  The frozen earth, and clothe in fresh attire
The lily and rose, that neither sowed nor spun.
What neat repast shall feast us, light and choice,
  Of Attic taste, with wine, whence we may rise
To hear the lute well touched, or artful voice
    Warble immortal notes and Tuscan air?
    He who of those delights can judge, and spare
To interpose them oft, is not unwise.

JOHN MILTON

To Cyriack Skinner

CYRIACK, whose grandsire on the royal bench
   Of British Themis, with no mean applause,
   Pronounced, and in his volumes taught, our Laws,
Which others at their Bar so often wrench,
To-day deep thoughts resolve with me to drench
   In mirth, that after no repenting draws;
   Let Euclid rest, and Archimedes pause,
And what the Swede intend, and what the French.
To measure life learn thou betimes, and know
   Toward solid good what leads the nearest way;
   For other things mild Heaven a time ordains,
And disapproves that care, though wise in show,
   That with superfluous burden loads the day,
     And, when God sends a cheerful hour, refrains.

JOHN MILTON

To the Same upon His Blindness

CYRIACK, this three years' day these eyes, though
  clear,
  To outward view, of blemish or of spot,
  Bereft of light, their seeing have forgot;
Nor to their idle orbs doth sight appear
Of sun, or moon, or star, throughout the year,
  Or man, or woman. Yet I argue not
  Against Heaven's hand or will, nor bate a jot
Of heart or hope; but still bear up and steer
Right onward. What supports me, dost thou ask?
  The conscience, friend, to have lost them overplied
In Liberty's defence, my noble task,
  Of which all Europe rings from side to side.
This thought might lead me through the world's
  vain mask
  Content, though blind, had I no better guide.

JOHN MILTON

On His Deceased Wife

METHOUGHT I saw my late espousèd saint
   Brought to me like Alcestis from the grave,
   Whom Jove's great son to her glad husband gave,
Rescued from Death by force, though pale and faint.
Mine, as whom washed from spot of child-bed taint
   Purification in the Old Law did save,
   And such as yet once more I trust to have
Full sight of her in Heaven without restraint,
Came vested all in white, pure as her mind.
   Her face was veiled; yet to my fancied sight
Love, sweetness, goodness, in her person shined
   So clear, as in no face with more delight.
But, oh! as to embrace me she inclined,
   I waked, she fled, and day brought back my night.

SIR RICHARD FANSHAWE
[1608-1666]

A Rose

Blown in the morning, thou shalt fade ere noon.
What boots a life which in such haste forsakes thee?
Thou'rt wondrous frolic, being to die so soon,
And passing proud a little colour makes thee.
If thee thy brittle beauty so deceives,
Know then the thing that swells thee is thy bane;
For the same beauty doth, in bloody leaves,
The sentence of thy early death contain.
Some clown's coarse lungs will poison thy sweet
    flower,
If by the careless plough thou shalt be torn;
And many Herods lie in wait each hour
To murder thee as soon as thou art born—
  Nay, force thy bud to blow—their tyrant breath
  Anticipating life, to hasten death!

THOMAS EDWARDS
[1699-1757]

To Richard Owen Cambridge

CAMBRIDGE, with whom, my pilot and my guide,
　Pleased I have traversed thy Sabrina's flood,
　Both where she foams impetuous, soiled with
　　mud,
And where she peaceful rolls her golden tide;
Never, oh, never let ambition's pride
　(Too oft pretexèd with our country's good),
　And tinselled pomp, despised when understood,
Or thirst of wealth, thee from her banks divide!
Reflect how calmly, like her infant wave,
　Flows the clear current of a private life;
　　See the wide public stream, by tempests tost,
Of every changing wind the sport or slave,
　Soiled with corruption, vexed with party strife,
　　Covered with wrecks of peace and honour lost.

THOMAS GRAY
[1716-1771]

On the Death of Richard West

In vain to me the smiling mornings shine,
  And reddening Phœbus lifts his golden fire;
The birds in vain their amorous descant join,
  Or cheerful fields resume their green attire:
These ears, alas! for other notes repine,
  A different object do these eyes require;
My lonely anguish melts no heart but mine,
  And in my breast the imperfect joys expire.
Yet morning smiles the busy race to cheer,
  And new-born pleasure brings to happier men;
The fields to all their wonted tribute bear,
  To warm their little loves the birds complain:
I fruitless mourn to him that cannot hear,
  And weep the more because I weep in vain.

THOMAS WARTON
[1728-1790]

On Bathing

WHEN late the trees were stript by Winter pale,
   Young Health, a dryad-maid in vesture green,
   Or like the forest's silver-quiver'd queen,
On airy uplands met the piercing gale;
And, ere its earliest echo shook the vale,
   Watching the hunter's joyous horn was seen.
   But since, gay-thron'd in fiery chariot sheen,
Summer has smote each daisy-dappled dale,
She to the cave retires, high-arched beneath
   The fount that laves proud Isis' towery brim;
And now all glad the temperate air to breathe,
   While cooling drops distil from arches dim,
Binding her dewy locks with sedgy wreath
   She sits amid the quire of Naiads trim.

WILLIAM COWPER
[1731-1800]

To Mrs. Unwin

MARY! I want a lyre with other strings,
 Such aid from heaven as some have feigned they
  drew,
 An eloquence scarce given to mortals, new
And undebased by praise of meaner things;
That, ere through age or woe I shed my wings,
 I may record thy worth with honour due,
 In verse as musical as thou art true,
And that immortalizes whom it sings.
But thou hast little need. There is a Book
 By seraphs writ with beams of heavenly light,
On which the eyes of God not rarely look,
 A chronicle of actions just and bright;—
  There all thy deeds, my faithful Mary, shine;
  And since thou own'st that praise, I spare thee
  mine.

JOHN CODRINGTON BAMFYLDE
[1754-1796]

On a Wet Summer

ALL ye who far from town in rural hall,
  Like me, were wont to dwell near pleasant field,
  Enjoying all the sunny day did yield,
With me the change lament, in irksome thrall,
By rains incessant held; for now no call
  From early swain invites my hand to wield
  The scythe. In parlour dim I sit concealed,
And mark the lessening sand from hour-glass fall;
Or 'neath my window view the wistful train
  Of dripping poultry, whom the vine's broad leaves
Shelter no more. Mute is the mournful plain;
    Silent the swallow sits beneath the thatch,
    And vacant hind hangs pensive o'er his hatch,
  Counting the frequent drips from reeded eaves.

THOMAS RUSSELL
[1762-1788]

Supposed to be Written at Lemnos

On this lone isle, whose rugged rocks affright
  The cautious pilot, ten revolving years
  Great Pæan's son, unwonted erst to tears,
Wept o'er his wound: alike each rolling light
Of heaven he watched, and blamed its lingering
    flight;
  By day the sea-mew screaming round his cave
  Drove slumber from his eyes; the chiding wave
And savage howlings chased his dreams by night.
Hope still was his: in each low breeze that sighed
  Through his rude grot he heard a coming oar,
In each white cloud a coming sail he spied;
  Nor seldom listened to the fancied roar
Of Œta's torrents, or the hoarser tide
  That parts famed Trachis from the Euboic shore.

SIR SAMUEL EGERTON BRYDGES
[1762-1837]

On Echo and Silence

IN eddying course when leaves began to fly,
  And Autumn in her lap the store to strew,
  As 'mid wild scenes I chanced the Muse to woo,
Through glens untrod and woods that frowned on
    high,
Two sleeping nymphs with wonder mute I spy!—
  And lo, she's gone!—in robe of dark green hue,
  'Twas Echo from her sister Silence flew:
For quick the hunter's horn resounded to the sky!
In shade affrighted Silence melts away.
  Not so her sister!—hark, for onward still
With far-heard step she takes her listening way,
  Bounding from rock to rock, and hill to hill!
Ah, mark the merry maid in mockful play
  With thousand mimic tones the laughing forest fill.

WILLIAM LISLE BOWLES
[1762-1850]

Ostend on Hearing the Bells at Sea

How sweet the tuneful bells' responsive peal!
  As when at opening dawn the fragrant breeze
  Touches the trembling sense of pale disease,
So piercing to my heart their force I feel.
  And hark! with lessening cadence now they fall
And now along the white and level tide
They fling their melancholy music wide;
  Bidding me many a tender thought recall
Of summer days, and those delightful years
  When by my native streams, in life's fair prime,
  The mournful magic of their mingling chime
First waked my wondering childhood into tears!
    But seeming now, when all those days are o'er,
    The sounds of joy once heard and heard no
    more.

WILLIAM LISLE BOWLES

Healing

O Time! who know'st a lenient hand to lay
   Softest on sorrow's wound, and slowly thence,
   Lulling to sad repose the weary sense,
The faint pang stealest unperceived away;
   On thee I rest my only hope at last,
And think, when thou hast dried the bitter tear
That flows in vain o'er all my soul held dear,
   I may look back on every sorrow past,
And meet life's peaceful evening with a smile;—
   As some lone bird, at day's departing hour,
   Sings in the sunbeam, of the transient shower
Forgetful, though its wings are wet the while:—
     Yet, ah! how much must that poor heart endure,
     Which hopes from thee, and thee alone, a cure!

WILLIAM WORDSWORTH
[1770-1850]

Of the Sonnet

NUNS fret not at their convent's narrow room;
  And hermits are contented with their cells,
  And students with their pensive citadels:
Maids at the wheel, the weaver at his loom,
Sit blithe and happy; bees that soar for bloom,
  High as the highest peak of Furness Fells,
  Will murmur by the hour in foxglove bells:
In truth the prison unto which we doom
Ourselves, no prison is: and hence for me,
  In sundry moods, 'twas pastime to be bound
  Within the sonnet's scanty plot of ground:
Pleased if some souls (for such there needs must be)
Who have felt the weight of too much liberty,
  Should find brief solace there, as I have found.

WILLIAM WORDSWORTH

Twilight

CALM is all nature as a resting wheel.
  The kine are couched upon the dewy grass;
  The horse alone, seen dimly as I pass,
Is cropping audibly his later meal:
Dark is the ground; a slumber seems to steal
  O'er vale, and mountain, and the starless sky.
  Now, in this blank of things, a harmony,
Home-felt, and home-created, seems to heal
  That grief for which the senses still supply
  Fresh food; for only then, when memory
Is hushed, am I at rest. My friends! restrain
Those busy cares that would allay my pain:
  Oh! leave me to myself; nor let me feel
The officious touch that makes me droop again.

WILLIAM WORDSWORTH

Composed upon Westminster Bridge
September 3, 1802

EARTH has not anything to show more fair:
    Dull would he be of soul who could pass by
    A sight so touching in its majesty:
This City now doth, like a garment, wear
The beauty of the morning; silent, bare,
    Ships, towers, domes, theatres, and temples lie
    Open unto the fields, and to the sky;
All bright and glittering in the smokeless air.
Never did sun more beautifully steep
    In his first splendour, valley, rock, or hill;
Ne'er saw I, never felt, a calm so deep!
    The river glideth at his own sweet will:
Dear God! the very houses seem asleep;
    And all that mighty heart is lying still!

WILLIAM WORDSWORTH

At Sunset

It is a beauteous Evening, calm and free,
    The holy time is quiet as a Nun
    Breathless with adoration; the broad sun
Is sinking down in its tranquillity;
The gentleness of heaven broods o'er the sea;
    Listen! the mighty Being is awake,
    And doth with his eternal motion make
A sound like thunder—everlastingly.
Dear Child! dear Girl! that walkest with me here,
    If thou appear untouched by solemn thought,
        Thy nature is not therefore less divine;
Thou liest in Abraham's bosom all the year;
        And worship'st at the Temple's inner shrine,
    God being with thee when we know it not.

WILLIAM WORDSWORTH

On the Extinction of the Venetian Republic

ONCE did She hold the gorgeous East in fee;
  And was the safeguard of the West: the worth
  Of Venice did not fall below her birth,
Venice, the eldest Child of Liberty.
She was a maiden City, bright and free:
  No guile seduced, no force could violate;
  And when she took unto herself a Mate,
She must espouse the everlasting Sea.
And what if she had seen those glories fade,
  Those titles vanish, and that strength decay?
Yet shall some tribute of regret be paid
  When her long life had reached its final day;
Men are we, and must grieve when even the Shade
  Of that which once was great is passed away.

WILLIAM WORDSWORTH

To Toussaint l'Ouverture

TOUSSAINT, the most unhappy man of men!
  Whether the whistling Rustic tend his plough
  Within thy hearing, or thy head be now
Pillowed in some deep dungeon's earless den;—
O miserable Chieftain! where and when
  Wilt thou find patience? Yet die not; do thou
  Wear rather in thy bonds a cheerful brow:
Though fallen thyself, never to rise again,
Live, and take comfort. Thou hast left behind
  Powers that will work for thee; air, earth, and skies;
There's not a breathing of the common wind
  That will forget thee; thou hast great allies;
  Thy friends are exultations, agonies,
And love, and man's unconquerable mind.

WILLIAM WORDSWORTH

Near Dover, September 1802

INLAND, within a hollow vale, I stood
   And saw, while sea was calm and air was clear,
   The coast of France—the coast of France how
      near!
Drawn almost into frightful neighbourhood.
I shrunk; for verily the barrier flood
   Was like a lake, or river bright and fair,
   A span of waters; yet what power is there!
What mightiness for evil and for good!
Even so doth God protect us if we be
   Virtuous and wise. Winds blow, and waters roll,
Strength to the brave, and Power, and Deity;
Yet in themselves are nothing! One decree
   Spake laws to *them*, and said that by the soul
Only, the Nations shall be great and free.

WILLIAM WORDSWORTH

Written in London, September 1802

O FRIEND! I know not which way I must look
   For comfort, being, as I am, opprest,
   To think that now our life is only drest
For show; mean handiwork of craftsman, cook,
Or groom!—We must run glittering like a brook
   In the open sunshine, or we are unblest:
   The wealthiest man among us is the best:
No grandeur now in nature or in book
Delights us. Rapine, avarice, expense,
   This is idolatry; and these we adore:
   Plain living and high thinking are no more;
   The homely beauty of the good old cause
Is gone; our peace, our fearful innocence,
    And pure religion breathing household laws.

WILLIAM WORDSWORTH

London 1802

I

MILTON! thou shouldst be living at this hour;
England hath need of thee; she is a fen
Of stagnant waters; altar, sword, and pen,
Fireside, the heroic wealth of hall and bower,
Have forfeited their ancient English dower
Of inward happiness. We are selfish men;
Oh! raise us up, return to us again;
And give us manners, virtue, freedom, power.
Thy soul was like a Star, and dwelt apart:
Thou hadst a voice whose sound was like the sea;
Pure as the naked heavens, majestic, free,
So didst thou travel on life's common way,
In cheerful godliness; and yet thy heart
The lowliest duties on herself did lay.

WILLIAM WORDSWORTH

London 1802

II

GREAT men have been among us; hands that penned
   And tongues that uttered wisdom—better none:
   The later Sidney, Marvell, Harrington,
Young Vane, and others who called Milton friend.
These moralists could act and comprehend:
   They knew how genuine glory was put on;
   Taught us how rightfully a nation shone
In splendour: what strength was that would not bend
But in magnanimous meekness. France, 'tis strange,
   Hath brought forth no such souls as we had then.
Perpetual emptiness! unceasing change!
   No single volume paramount, no code,
   No master spirit, no determined road;
   But equally a want of books and men!

WILLIAM WORDSWORTH

London 1802

III

It is not to be thought of that the Flood
  Of British freedom, which, to the open sea
  Of the world's praise, from dark antiquity
Hath flowed, "with pomp of waters, unwithstood,"
Roused though it be full often to a mood
  Which spurns the check of salutary bands,—
  That this most famous Stream in bogs and sands
Should perish; and to evil and to good
Be lost for ever. In our halls is hung
  Armoury of the invincible Knights of old:
We must be free or die, who speak the tongue
  That Shakespeare spake; the faith and morals hold
Which Milton held.—In every thing we are sprung
  Of Earth's first blood, have titles manifold.

WILLIAM WORDSWORTH

London 1802

I V

WHEN I have borne in memory what has tamed
   Great nations, how ennobling thoughts depart
   When men change swords for ledgers, and desert
The student's bower for gold, some fears unnamed
I had, my country!—am I to be blamed?
   But when I think of thee, and what thou art,
   Verily, in the bottom of my heart,
Of those unfilial fears I am ashamed.
But dearly must we prize thee; we who find
   In thee a bulwark for the cause of men;
     And I by my affection was beguiled.
What wonder if a poet now and then,
Among the many movements of his mind,
     Felt for thee as a lover or a child?

WILLIAM WORDSWORTH

Worldliness

THE world is too much with us; late and soon,
    Getting and spending, we lay waste our powers:
    Little we see in Nature that is ours;
We have given our hearts away, a sordid boon!
This Sea that bares her bosom to the moon;
    The winds that will be howling at all hours,
    And are up-gathered now like sleeping flowers;
For this, for every thing, we are out of tune;
It moves us not.—Great God! I'd rather be
    A Pagan suckled in a creed outworn;
So might I, standing on this pleasant lea,
    Have glimpses that would make me less forlorn;
Have sight of Proteus rising from the sea;
    Or hear old Triton blow his wreathèd horn.

WILLIAM WORDSWORTH

Two Ships

I

WITH ships the sea was sprinkled far and nigh,
  Like stars in heaven, and joyously it showed;
  Some lying fast at anchor in the road,
Some veering up and down, one knew not why.
A goodly vessel did I then espy
  Come like a giant from a haven broad;
  And lustily along the bay she strode,
Her tackling rich, and of apparel high.
This ship was nought to me, nor I to her,
  Yet I pursued her with a Lover's look;
This ship to all the rest did I prefer:
  When will she turn, and whither? She will brook
No tarrying; where She comes the winds must stir:
  On went She,—and due north her journey took.

WILLIAM WORDSWORTH

Two Ships

I I

WHERE lies the land to which yon ship must go?
   Fresh as a lark mounting at break of day
   Festively she puts forth in trim array;
Is she for tropic suns, or polar snow?
What boots the inquiry?—Neither friend nor foe
   She cares for; let her travel where she may,
   She finds familiar names, a beaten way
Ever before her, and a wind to blow.
Yet still I ask, what haven is her mark?
   And, almost as it was when ships were rare,
   (From time to time, like pilgrims, here and there
Crossing the waters) doubt, and something dark,
   Of the old sea some reverential fear,
Is with me at thy farewell, joyous bark!

WILLIAM WORDSWORTH

1807

Thought of a Briton on the Subjugation of Switzerland

Two Voices are there; one is of the Sea,
   One of the Mountains; each a mighty Voice:
   In both from age to age thou didst rejoice,
They were thy chosen music, Liberty!
There came a Tyrant, and with holy glee
   Thou foughtst against him; but hast vainly striven:
   Thou from thy Alpine holds at length art driven,
Where not a torrent murmurs heard by thee.
Of one deep bliss thine ear hath been bereft:
Then cleave, O cleave to that which still is left;
   For, high-souled Maid, what sorrow would it be
That Mountain floods should thunder as before,
And Ocean bellow from his rocky shore,
   And neither awful Voice be heard by thee!

WILLIAM WORDSWORTH

Of His Daughter Catherine
Dead Long Since

SURPRISED by joy—impatient as the Wind
  I turned to share the transport—Oh! with whom
  But Thee, deep buried in the silent tomb,
That spot which no vicissitude can find?
Love, faithful love, recalled thee to my mind—
  But how could I forget thee?—Through what
    power,
  Even for the least division of an hour,
Have I been so beguiled as to be blind
To my most grievous loss!—That thought's return
  Was the worst pang that sorrow ever bore,
Save one, one only, when I stood forlorn,
  Knowing my heart's best treasure was no more;
That neither present time, nor years unborn,
  Could to my sight that heavenly face restore.

WILLIAM WORDSWORTH

After-thought (*River Duddon*)

I THOUGHT of Thee, my partner and my guide,
    As being past away.—Vain sympathies!
    For, backward, Duddon, as I cast my eyes,
I see what was, and is, and will abide;
Still glides the Stream, and shall for ever glide;
    The Form remains, the Function never dies;
    While we, the brave, the mighty, and the wise,
We Men, who in our morn of youth defied
The elements, must vanish;—be it so!
    Enough, if something from our hands have power
    To live, and act, and serve the future hour;
And if, as toward the silent tomb we go,
    Through love, through hope, and faith's tran-
        scendent dower,
We feel that we are greater than we know.

WILLIAM WORDSWORTH

Inside of King's College Chapel, Cambridge

TAX not the royal Saint with vain expense,
   With ill-matched aims the Architect who planned—
   Albeit labouring for a scanty band
Of white-robed Scholars only—this immense
And glorious work of fine intelligence!
   Give all thou canst; high Heaven rejects the lore
   Of nicely-calculated less or more;
So deemed the man who fashioned for the sense
These lofty pillars, spread that branching roof
   Self-poised, and scooped into ten thousand cells,
   Where light and shade repose, where music dwells
   Lingering—and wandering on as loth to die;
Like thoughts whose very sweetness yieldeth proof
   That they were born for immortality.

WILLIAM WORDSWORTH

Mutability

FROM low to high doth dissolution climb,
    And sink from high to low, along a scale
    Of awful notes, whose concord shall not fail;
A musical but melancholy chime,
Which they can hear who meddle not with crime,
    Nor avarice, nor over-anxious care.
    Truth fails not; but her outward forms that bear
The longest date do melt like frosty rime,
That in the morning whitened hill and plain
    And is no more; drop like the tower sublime
        Of yesterday, which royally did wear
Its crown of weeds, but could not even sustain
      Some casual shout that broke the silent air,
    Or the unimaginable touch of Time.

WILLIAM WORDSWORTH

The Trossachs

THERE's not a nook within this solemn Pass,
　　But were an apt confessional for One
　　Taught by his summer spent, his autumn gone,
That Life is but a tale of morning grass
Withered at eve. From scenes of art which chase
　　That thought away, turn, and with watchful eyes
　　Feed it 'mid Nature's old felicities,
Rocks, rivers, and smooth lakes more clear than glass
Untouched, unbreathed upon. Thrice happy quest,
　　If from a golden perch of aspen spray
　　(October's workmanship to rival May)
The pensive warbler of the ruddy breast
　　That moral sweeten by a heaven-taught lay,
Lulling the year, with all its cares, to rest.

WILLIAM WORDSWORTH

In Sight of the Town of Cockermouth, where the
Author was Born, and His Father's Remains are Laid

A POINT of life between my Parent's dust,
   And yours, my buried Little-ones! am I;
   And to those graves looking habitually
In kindred quiet I repose my trust.
Death to the innocent is more than just,
   And, to the sinner, mercifully bent;
   So may I hope, if truly I repent
And meekly bear the ills which bear I must:
And You, my Offspring! that do still remain,
   Yet may outstrip me in the appointed race,
If e'er, through fault of mine, in mutual pain
   We breathed together for a moment's space,
The wrong, by love provoked, let love arraign,
   And only love keep in your hearts a place.

WILLIAM WORDSWORTH

Mary Queen of Scots
Landing at the Mouth of the Derwent, Workington

DEAR to the Loves, and to the Graces vowed,
  The Queen drew back the wimple that she wore;
  And to the throng, that on the Cumbrian shore
Her landing hailed, how touchingly she bowed;
Bright as a Star (that, from a sombre cloud
  Of pine-tree foliage poised in air, forth darts,
  When a soft summer gale at evening parts
The gloom that did its loveliness enshroud)
She smiled; but Time, the old Saturnian seer,
  Sighed on the wing as her foot pressed the strand,
    With step prelusive to a long array
  Of woes and degradations hand in hand,
Weeping captivity, and shuddering fear
    Stilled by the ensanguined block of Fotheringay!

WILLIAM WORDSWORTH

Walk in Meditation

MOST sweet it is with unuplifted eyes
    To pace the ground, if path there be or none,
While a fair region round the traveller lies,
    Which he forbears again to look upon;
Pleased rather with some soft ideal scene,
    The work of Fancy or some happy tone
Of meditation, slipping in between
    The beauty coming and the beauty gone.
If Thought and Love desert us, from that day
    Let us break off all commerce with the Muse;
With Thought and Love companions of our way,
    Whate'er the senses take or may refuse,
    The Mind's internal heaven shall shed her dews
Of inspiration on the humblest lay.

WILLIAM WORDSWORTH

WHY art thou silent? Is thy love a plant
  Of such weak fibre that the treacherous air
  Of absence withers what was once so fair?
Is there no debt to pay, no boon to grant?
Yet have my thoughts for thee been vigilant—
  Bound to thy service with unceasing care,
The mind's least generous wish a mendicant
  For naught but what thy happiness could spare.
Speak, though this soft warm heart, once free to hold
  A thousand tender pleasures, thine and mine,
Be left more desolate, more dreary cold
    Than a forsaken bird's-nest filled with snow
    'Mid its own bush of leafless eglantine;
    Speak, that my torturing doubts their end may
      know!

WILLIAM WORDSWORTH

Composed on a May Morning, 1838

LIFE with yon Lambs, like day, is just begun,
  Yet nature seems to them a heavenly guide.
  Does joy approach? they meet the coming tide;
And sullenness avoid, as now they shun
Pale twilight's lingering glooms,—and in the sun
  Couch near their dams, with quiet satisfied;
  Or gambol—each with his shadow at his side,
Varying its shape wherever he may run.
As they from turf yet hoar with sleepy dew
  All turn, and court the shining and the green,
  Where herbs look up, and opening flowers are
    seen;
Why to God's goodness cannot We be true,
  And so, His gifts and promises between,
Feed to the last on pleasures ever new?

WILLIAM WORDSWORTH

Ministration

Though the bold wings of Poesy affect
  The clouds, and wheel around the mountain tops
  Rejoicing, from her loftiest height she drops
Well pleased to skim the plain with wild flowers deckt,
Or muse in solemn grove whose shades protect
  The lingering dew—there steals along, or stops,
  Watching the least small bird that round her hops,
Or creeping worm, with sensitive respect.
Her functions are they therefore less divine,
  Her thoughts less deep, or void of grave intent
Her simplest fancies? Should that fear be thine,
  Aspiring Votary, ere thy hand present
One offering, kneel before her modest shrine
  With brow in penitential sorrow bent!

SAMUEL TAYLOR COLERIDGE
[1772-1834]

To Nature

It may indeed be phantasy when I
   Essay to draw from all created things
   Deep, heartfelt, inward joy that closely clings;
And trace in leaves and flowers that round me lie
Lessons of love and earnest piety.
   So let it be; and if the wide world rings
   In mock of this belief, to me it brings
Nor fear, nor grief, nor vain perplexity.
So will I build my altar in the fields,
   And the blue sky my fretted dome shall be,
And the sweet fragrance that the wild flower yields
   Shall be the incense I will yield to Thee,
      Thee only God! and Thou shalt not despise
      Even me, the priest of this poor sacrifice.

SAMUEL TAYLOR COLERIDGE

Fancy in Nubibus, or the Poet in the Cloud

O IT is pleasant, with a heart at ease,
    Just after sunset, or by moonlight skies,
To make the shifting clouds be what you please,
    Or let the easily-persuaded eyes
Own each quaint likeness issuing from the mould
    Of a friend's fancy; or, with head bent low
And cheek aslant, see rivers flow of gold
      'Twixt crimson banks; and then, a traveller, go
From mount to mount through Cloudland, gorgeous
      land!
    Or listening to the tide, with closèd sight,
Be that blind bard who, on the Chian strand
    By those deep sounds possessed with inward light,
      Beheld the Iliad and the Odyssee
      Rise to the swelling of the voiceful sea.

SAMUEL TAYLOR COLERIDGE

Work without Hope

ALL Nature seems at work. Slugs leave their lair—
The bees are stirring—birds are on the wing—
And Winter, slumbering in the open air,
Wears on his smiling face a dream of Spring!
And I, the while, the sole unbusy thing,
Nor honey make, nor pair, nor build, nor sing.

Yet well I ken the banks where amaranths blow,
Have traced the fount whence streams of nectar flow.
Bloom, O ye amaranths! bloom for whom ye may,
For me ye bloom not! Glide, rich streams, away!
With lips unbrighten'd, wreathless brow, I stroll:
And would you learn the spells that drowse my soul?
Work without Hope draws nectar in a sieve,
And Hope without an object cannot live.

CHARLES LAMB
[1775-1834]

A Missal

O LIFT with reverent hand that tarnished flower,
  That shrines beneath her modest canopy,
  Memorials dear to Romish piety,—
Dim specks, rude shapes, of Saints! in fervent hour
  The work perchance of some weak devotee
Who, poor in worldly treasures to set forth
The sanctities she worshipped to their worth,
  In this imperfect tracery might see
Hints, that all Heaven did to her sense reveal.
  Cheap gifts best fit poor givers. We are told
  Of the lone mite, the cup of water cold,
That in their way approved the offerer's zeal.
    True Love shows costliest where the means are
      scant;
    And, in her reckoning, they *abound* who *want*.

JOSEPH BLANCO WHITE
[1775-1841]

Night and Death

MYSTERIOUS Night! when our first parent knew
  Thee from report divine, and heard thy name,
  Did he not tremble for this lovely frame,
This glorious canopy of light and blue.
Yet 'neath a curtain of translucent dew,
  Bathed in the rays of the great setting flame,
  Hesperus with the host of heaven came,
And lo! creation widened in man's view.
Who could have thought such darkness lay concealed
  Within thy beams, O Sun! or who could find,
Whilst fly and leaf and insect stood revealed,
   That to such countless orbs thou mad'st us blind!
    Why do we then shun Death with anxious strife?
    If Light can thus deceive, wherefore not Life?

LEIGH HUNT
[1784-1859]

To the Grasshopper and the Cricket

GREEN little vaulter in the sunny grass,
 Catching your heart up at the feel of June,
 Sole voice that's heard amidst the lazy noon,
When even the bees lag at the summoning brass;
And you, warm little housekeeper, who class
 With those who think the candles come too soon,
 Loving the fire, and with your tricksome tune
Nick the glad silent moments as they pass;
O, sweet and tiny cousins! that belong,
 One to the fields, the other to the hearth,
Both have your sunshine; both though small are
  strong
 At your clear hearts; and both were sent on earth
To sing in thoughtful ears this natural song:
 In doors and out, summer and winter, Mirth.

LEIGH HUNT

The Nile

IT flows through all hushed Ægypt and its sands,
   Like some grave mighty thought threading a dream,
   And times and things, as in that vision seem
Keeping along it their eternal stands,
Caves, pillars, pyramids, the shepherd bands
   That roamed through the young world, the glory
      extreme
   Of high Sesostris, and that southern beam,
The laughing queen that caught the world's great
      hands.
Then comes a mightier silence, stern and strong,
As of a world left empty of its throng,
   And the void weighs on us; and then we wake,
And hear the fruitful stream lapsing along
    'Twixt villages, and think how we shall take
    Our own calm journey on for human sake.

LEIGH HUNT

The Fish, the Man, and the Spirit

To Fish

You strange, astonished looking, angle-faced,
Dreary-mouthed, gaping wretches of the sea,
Gulping salt-water everlastingly,
Cold-blooded, though with red your blood be graced,
And mute, though dwellers in the roaring waste;
And you, all shapes beside, that fishy be,—
Some round, some flat, some long, all devilry,
Legless, unloving, infamously chaste:—

O scaly, slippery, wet, swift, staring wights,
What is't ye do? What life lead? eh, dull goggles?
How do ye vary your vile days and nights?
How pass your Sundays? Are ye still but joggles
In ceaseless wash? Still nought but gapes, and bites,
And drinks, and stares, diversified with boggles?

LEIGH HUNT

A Fish Answers

AMAZING monster! that, for aught I know,
With the first sight of thee didst make our race
For ever stare! O flat and shocking face,
Grimly divided from the breast below!
Thou that on dry land horribly dost go
With a split body and most ridiculous pace,
Prong after prong, disgracer of all grace,
Long useless-finned, haired, upright, unwet, slow!

O breather of unbreathable, sword-sharp air,
How canst exist? How bear thyself, thou dry
And dreary sloth! What particle canst share
Of the only blessed life, the watery?
I sometimes see of ye an actual *pair*
Go by! linked fin by fin! most odiously.

LEIGH HUNT

*The Fish turned into a Man, and then into a Spirit,
and again Speaks*

INDULGE thy smiling scorn, if smiling still,
O man! and loathe, but with a sort of love:
For difference must its use by difference prove,
And, in sweet clang, the spheres with music fill.
One of the spirits am I, that at his will
Live in whate'er has life—fish, eagle, dove—
No hate, no pride, beneath nought, nor above,
A visitor of the rounds of God's sweet skill.

Man's life is warm, glad, sad, 'twixt loves and graves,
Boundless in hope, honoured with pangs austere,
Heaven-gazing; and his angel-wings he craves:—
The fish is swift, small-needing, vague yet clear,
A cold, sweet, silver life, wrapped in round waves,
Quickened with touches of transporting fear.

GEORGE GORDON, LORD BYRON
[1788-1824]

On Chillon

ETERNAL Spirit of the chainless Mind!
   Brightest in dungeons, Liberty, thou art—
   For there thy habitation is the heart—
The heart which love of thee alone can bind;
And when thy sons to fetters are consigned,
   To fetters, and the damp vault's dayless gloom,
   Their country conquers with their martyrdom,
And Freedom's fame finds wings on every wind.
Chillon! thy prison is a holy place,
   And thy sad floor an altar, for 'twas trod,
Until his very steps have left a trace
   Worn as if thy cold pavement were a sod,
By Bonnivard! May none those marks efface!
   For they appeal from tyranny to God.

SIR AUBREY DE VERE
[1788-1846]

The "Children's Crusade"

ALL holy influences dwell within
   The breast of Childhood: instincts fresh from God
   Inspire it, ere the heart beneath the rod
Of grief hath bled, or caught the plague of sin.
How mighty was that fervour which could win
   Its way to infant souls!—and was the sod
   Of Palestine by infant Croises trod?
Like Joseph went they forth, or Benjamin,
In all their touching beauty, to redeem?
   And did their soft lips kiss the sepulchre?
Alas! the lovely pageant, as a dream,
   Faded! they sank not through ignoble fear;
They felt not Moslem steel. By mountain, stream,
   In sands, in fens, they died—no mother near!

PERCY BYSSHE SHELLEY
[1792-1822]

Ozymandias

I MET a traveller from an antique land
   Who said: Two vast and trunkless legs of stone
Stand in the desert. Near them, on the sand,
   Half sunk, a shattered visage lies, whose frown
And wrinkled lip and sneer of cold command
   Tell that its sculptor well those passions read
Which yet survive, stamped on these lifeless things,
   The hand that mocked them and the heart that
      fed;
   And on the pedestal these words appear:
"My name is Ozymandias, king of kings:
   Look on my works, ye Mighty, and despair!"
Nothing beside remains. Round the decay
   Of that colossal wreck, boundless and bare
The lone and level sands stretch far away.

JOHN KEBLE
[1792-1866]

At Hooker's Tomb

THE grey-eyed Morn was saddened with a shower,
   A silent shower, that trickled down so still
Scarce dropped beneath its weight the tenderest
      flower,
   Scarce could you trace it on the twinkling rill,
Or moss-stone bathed in dew. It was an hour
   Most meet for prayer beside thy lowly grave,
Most for thanksgiving meet, that Heaven such power
   To thy serene and humble spirit gave.
"Who sow good seed with tears shall reap in joy."
   So thought I as I watched the gracious rain,
And deemed it like that silent sad employ
      Whence sprung thy glory's harvest, to remain
      For ever. God hath sworn to lift on high
      Who sinks himself by true humility.

FELICIA DOROTHEA HEMANS
[1794-1835]

Flight of the Spirit

WHITHER, oh! whither wilt thou wing thy way?
　What solemn region first upon thy sight
　Shall break, unveiled for terror or delight?
What hosts, magnificent in dread array,
My spirit! when thy prison-house of clay
　After long strife is rent? Fond, fruitless quest!
　The unfledged bird, within his narrow nest,
Sees but a few green branches o'er him play,
And through their parting leaves, by fits revealed,
A glimpse of summer sky; nor knows the field
　Wherein his dormant powers must yet be tried.
　　Thou art that bird!—of what beyond thee lies
　　Far in the untracked, immeasurable skies
Knowing but this—that thou shalt find thy Guide!

JOHN KEATS
[1796-1821]

On First Looking into Chapman's Homer

MUCH have I travelled in the realms of gold
 And many goodly states and kingdoms seen;
 Round many western islands have I been
Which bards in fealty to Apollo hold.
Oft of one wide expanse had I been told
 That deep-browed Homer ruled as his demesne;
 Yet did I never breathe its pure serene
Till I heard Chapman speak out loud and bold.
Then felt I like some watcher of the skies
 When a new planet swims into his ken;
Or like stout Cortez, when with eagle eyes
 He stared at the Pacific—and all his men
Looked at each other with a wild surmise—
 Silent, upon a peak in Darien.

JOHN KEATS

On the Grasshopper and Cricket

THE poetry of earth is never dead:
    When all the birds are faint with the hot sun,
    And hide in cooling trees, a voice will run
From hedge to hedge about the new-mown mead;
That is the Grasshopper's—he takes the lead
    In summer luxury—he has never done
    With his delights; for when tired out with fun,
He rests at ease beneath some pleasant weed.
The poetry of earth is ceasing never:
    On a lone winter evening, when the frost
      Has wrought a silence, from the stove there shrills
The Cricket's song, in warmth increasing ever,
    And seems, to one in drowsiness half lost,
      The Grasshopper's among some grassy hills.

JOHN KEATS

To Homer

STANDING aloof in giant ignorance
　　Of thee I hear and of the Cyclades,
As one who sits ashore and longs perchance
　　To visit dolphin-coral in deep seas.
So thou wast blind;—but then the veil was rent,
　　For Jove uncurtain'd Heaven to let thee live,
And Neptune made for thee a spumy tent,
　　And Pan made sing for thee his forest-hive;
Aye on the shores of darkness there is light,
　　And precipices show untrodden green,
There is a budding morrow in midnight,
　　There is a triple sight in blindness keen;
Such seeing hadst thou, as it once befel
To Dian, Queen of Earth, and Heaven, and Hell.

JOHN KEATS

To Ailsa Rock

HEARKEN, thou craggy ocean pyramid!
  Give answer from thy voice, the sea-fowl's screams!
  When were thy shoulders mantled in huge streams?
When, from the sun, was thy broad forehead hid?
How long is't since the mighty power bid
  Thee heave to airy sleep from fathom dreams?
  Sleep in the lap of thunder or sun-beams,
Or when grey clouds are thy cold cover-lid?
Thou answer'st not, for thou art dead asleep!
  Thy life is but two dead eternities—
The last in air, the former in the deep;
  First with the whales, last with the eagle-skies—
Drown'd wast thou till earthquake made thee steep,
  Another cannot wake thy giant size.

JOHN KEATS

Fame

"You cannot eat your cake and have it too!"—*Proverb*

How fever'd is the man, who cannot look
   Upon his mortal days with temperate blood,
Who vexes all the leaves of his life's book,
   And robs his fair name of its maidenhood;
It is as if the rose should pluck herself,
   Or the ripe plum finger its misty bloom,
As if a Naiad, like a meddling elf,
   Should darken her pure grot with muddy gloom,
But the rose leaves herself upon the briar,
   For winds to kiss and grateful bees to feed,
And the ripe plum still wears its dim attire,
     The undisturbed lake has crystal space,
     Why then should man, teasing the world for
      grace,
   Spoil his salvation for a fierce miscreed?

JOHN KEATS

The Sonnet Claims more Freedom

IF by dull rhymes our English must be chained,
  And, like Andromeda, the Sonnet sweet
Fettered, in spite of painèd loveliness;
Let us find out if we must be constrained,
  Sandals more interwoven and complete
To fit the naked foot of poesy;
Let us inspect the lyre, and weigh the stress
Of every chord, and see what may be gained
  By ear industrious, and attention meet;
Misers of sound and syllable, no less
Than Midas of his coinage, let us be
  Jealous of dead leaves in that bay wreath crown;
So, if we may not let the Muse be free,
  She will be bound with garlands of her own.

JOHN KEATS

To Sleep

O soft embalmer of the still midnight!
  Shutting with careful fingers and benign,
Our gloom-pleased eyes, embowered from the light,
  Enshaded in forgetfulness divine;
O soothest Sleep! if so it please thee, close,
  In midst of this thine hymn, my willing eyes,
Or wait the amen, ere thy poppy throws
  Around my bed its lulling charities;
  Then save me, or the passèd day will shine
Upon my pillow, breeding many woes;
  Save me from curious conscience, that still lords
Its strength, for darkness burrowing like a mole;
  Turn the key deftly in the oilèd wards,
And seal the hushèd casket of my soul.

JOHN KEATS

Keats' Last Sonnet

BRIGHT *Star!* would I were steadfast as thou art—
  Not in lone splendour hung aloft the night,
And watching with eternal lids apart,
  Like Nature's patient, sleepless Eremite,
The moving waters at their priest-like task
  Of pure ablution round earth's human shores,
Or gazing on the new soft fallen mask
  Of snow upon the mountains and the moors—
No—yet still steadfast, still unchangeable,
  Pillowed upon my fair love's ripening breast,
To feel for ever its soft fall and swell,
  Awake for ever in a sweet unrest,
Still, still to hear her tender-taken breath,
And so live ever—or else swoon to death.

HARTLEY COLERIDGE
[1796-1849]

Prayer

Be not afraid to pray—to pray is right.
  Pray, if thou canst, with hope; but ever pray,
  Though hope be weak, or sick with long delay;
Pray in the darkness, if there be no light.
Far is the time, remote from human sight,
  When war and discord on the earth shall cease;
  Yet every prayer for universal peace
Avails the blessèd time to expedite.
Whate'er is good to wish, ask that of Heaven,
  Though it be what thou canst not hope to see:
Pray to be perfect, though material leaven
  Forbid the spirit so on earth to be;
But if for any wish thou darest not pray,
Then pray to God to cast that wish away.

Friendship

WHEN we were idlers with the loitering rills,
  The need of human love we little noted:
  Our love was nature; and the peace that floated
On the white mist, and dwelt upon the hills,
To sweet accord subdued our wayward wills:
  One soul was ours, one mind, one heart devoted,
  That, wisely doting, ask'd not why it doted,
And ours the unknown joy, which knowing kills.
But now I find how dear thou wert to me;
  That man is more than half of nature's treasure,
Of that fair beauty which no eye can see,
  Of that sweet music which no eye can measure;
  And now the streams may sing for others' pleasure,
The hills sleep on in their eternity.

THOMAS HOOD
[1798-1845]

Silence

THERE is a silence where hath been no sound;
  There is a silence where no sound may be
  In the cold grave—under the deep, deep sea,
Or in wide desert where no life is found,
Which hath been mute, and still must sleep profound;
  No voice is hushed—not life treads silently,
  But clouds and cloudy shadows wander free
That never spoke, over the idle ground.
But in green ruins, in the desolate walls
  Of antique palaces, where Man hath been,
Though the dun fox, or wild hyæna, calls,
  And owls, that flit continually between,
Shriek to the echo, and the low winds moan.
There the true Silence is, self-conscious and alone.

THOMAS HOOD

Death

IT is not death, that sometime in a sigh
   This eloquent breath shall take its speechless flight;
That sometime these bright stars, that now reply
   In sunlight to the sun, shall set in night,
   That this warm conscious flesh shall perish quite,
And all life's ruddy springs forget to flow;
   That thoughts shall cease, and the immortal sprite
Be lapped in alien clay and laid below;
It is not death to know this,—but to know
   That pious thoughts, which visit at new graves
In tender pilgrimage, will cease to go
   So duly and so oft,—and when grass waves
Over the past-away, there may be then
No resurrection in the minds of men.

SAMUEL LAMAN BLANCHARD
[1804-1845]

Wishes of Youth

GAILY and greenly let my seasons run:
  And should the war-winds of the world uproot
  The sanctities of life, and its sweet fruit
Cast forth as fuel for the fiery sun;
The dews be turned to ice—fair days begun
  In peace wear out in pain, and sounds that suit
  Despair and discord keep Hope's harpstring mute;
Still let me live as Love and Life were one:
Still let me turn on earth a child-like gaze,
  And trust the whispered charities that bring
Tidings of human truth; with inward praise
  Watch the weak motion of each common thing
And find it glorious—still let me raise
  On wintry wrecks an altar to the Spring.

SIR WILLIAM ROWAN HAMILTON
[1805-1865]

Spirit of Wisdom and of Love

O BROODING Spirit of Wisdom and of Love,
   Whose mighty wings even now o'ershadow me;
   Absorb me in thine own immensity,
And raise me far my finite self above!
Purge vanity away and the weak care
   That name or fame of me should widely spread;
   And the deep wish keep burning in their stead
Thy blissful influence afar to bear,
Or see it borne! Let no desire of ease,
   No lack of courage, faith, or love, delay
   My own steps in that high thought-paven way,
In which my soul her clear commission sees:
   Yet with an equal joy let me behold
   Thy chariot o'er that way by others roll'd.

ELIZABETH BARRETT BROWNING
[1806-1861]

Grief

I TELL you, hopeless grief is passionless;
  That only men incredulous of despair,
  Half-taught in anguish, through the midnight air
Beat upward to God's throne in loud access
Of shrieking and reproach. Full desertness
  In souls as countries, lieth silent-bare
  Under the blanching vertical eye-glare
Of the absolute Heavens. Deep-hearted man, express
Grief for thy Dead in silence like to death—
  Most like a monumental statue set
    In everlasting watch and moveless woe,
Till itself crumble to the dust beneath.
  Touch it; the marble eyelids are not wet:
    If it could weep, it would arise and go.

ELIZABETH BARRETT BROWNING

Sonnets from the Portuguese

I

BUT only three in all God's universe
  Have heard this word thou hast said; Himself,
    beside
  Thee speaking and me listening! and replied
One of us . . . *that* was God! . . . and laid the curse
So darkly on my eyelids as to amerce
  My sight from seeing thee—that if I had died,
  The deathweights, placed there, would have signi-
    fied
Less absolute exclusion. "Nay" is worse
From God than from all others, O my friend!
  Men could not part us with their worldly jars,
Nor the seas change us, nor the tempests bend;
  Our hands would touch, for all the mountain-bars;
And, heaven being rolled between us at the end,
  We should but vow the faster for the stars.

ELIZABETH BARRETT BROWNING

I I

UNLIKE are we, unlike, O princely Heart!
　Unlike our uses, and our destinies.
　Our ministering two angels look surprise
On one another, as they strike athwart
Their wings in passing. Thou, bethink thee, art
　A guest for queens to social pageantries
　With gages from a hundred brighter eyes
Than tears, even, can make mine, to ply thy part
Of chief musician. What hast *thou* to do
　With looking from the lattice-lights at me,
A poor, tired, wandering singer? . . . singing through
　The dark, and leaning up a cypress tree?
The chrism is on thine head,—on mine, the dew—
　And Death must dig the level where these agree.

ELIZABETH BARRETT BROWNING

III

Go from me. Yet I feel that I shall stand
   Henceforward in thy shadow. Nevermore
   Alone upon the threshold of my door
Of individual life, shall I command
The uses of my soul, nor lift my hand
   Serenely in the sunshine as before,
   Without the sense of that which I forebore . . .
Thy touch upon the palm. The widest land
Doom takes to part us, leaves thy heart in mine
   With pulses that beat double. What I do
And what I dream include thee, as the wine
   Must taste of its own grapes. And when I sue
God for myself, He hears that name of thine,
   And sees within my eyes, the tears of two.

ELIZABETH BARRETT BROWNING

V

If thou must love me, let it be for nought
Except for love's sake only. Do not say,
"I love her for her smile . . . her look . . . her way
Of speaking gently, . . . for a trick of thought
That falls in well with mine, and certes brought
A sense of pleasant ease on such a day"—
For these things in themselves, Beloved, may
Be changed, or change for thee,—and love so wrought
May be unwrought so. Neither love me for
Thine own dear pity's wiping my cheeks dry,
Since one might well forget to weep who bore
Thy comfort long, and lose thy love thereby,
But love me for love's sake, that evermore
Thou mayst love on through love's eternity.

ELIZABETH BARRETT BROWNING

VI

WHEN our two souls stand up erect and strong,
    Face to face, silent, drawing nigh and nigher,
    Until the lengthening wings break into fire
At either curvèd point,—what bitter wrong
Can the earth do us, that we should not long
    Be here contented? Think. In mounting higher
    The angels would press on us, and aspire
To drop some golden orb of perfect song
Into our deep, dear silence. Let us stay
    Rather on earth, Beloved,—where the unfit
Contrarious moods of men recoil away
    And isolate pure spirits, and permit
A place to stand and love in for a day,
    With darkness and the death-hour rounding it.

HENRY WADSWORTH LONGFELLOW
[1807-1882]

Chaucer

An old man in a lodge within a park;
  The chamber walls depicted all around
  With portraitures of huntsman, hawk, and hound,
And the hurt deer. He listeneth to the lark,
Whose song comes with the sunshine through the dark
  Of painted glass in leaden lattice bound;
  He listeneth and he laugheth at the sound,
Then writeth in a book like any clerk.
He is the poet of the dawn, who wrote
  The Canterbury Tales, and his old age
    Made beautiful with song; and as I read
I hear the crowing cock, I hear the note
  Of lark and linnet, and from every page
    Rise odours of plough'd field or flowery mead.

HENRY WADSWORTH LONGFELLOW

Divina Commedia

(Prefixed to his translation of it)

OFT have I seen at some cathedral door
　A labourer, pausing in the dust and heat,
　Lay down his burden, and with reverent feet
Enter, and cross himself, and on the floor
Kneel to repeat his Paternoster o'er:
　Far off the noises of the world retreat—
　The loud vociferations of the street
Become an indistinguishable roar.
So, as I enter here from day to day,
　And leave my burden at this minster gate,
Kneeling in prayer, and not ashamed to pray,
　The tumult of the time disconsolate
To inarticulate murmurs dies away,
　While the eternal ages watch and wait.

Nature

As a fond mother, when the day is o'er,
  Leads by the hand her little child to bed,
  Half willing, half reluctant to be led
And leave his broken playthings on the floor,
Still gazing at them through the open door,
  Not wholly reassured and comforted
  By promises of others in their stead,
Which, though more splendid, may not please him
    more;
So Nature deals with us, and takes away
  Our playthings one by one, and by the hand
  Leads us to rest so gently that we go
Scarce knowing if we wish to go or stay,
  Being too full of sleep to understand
    How the unknown transcends the what we know.

CHARLES TENNYSON TURNER
[1808-1879]

Letty's Globe

WHEN Letty had scarce passed her third glad year,
    And her young artless words began to flow,
One day we gave the child a coloured sphere
    Of the wide earth, that she might mark and know,
By tint and outline, all its sea and land.
    She patted all the world; old empires peeped
Between her baby fingers; her soft hand
    Was welcome at all frontiers. How she leaped,
    And laughed and prattled in her world-wide bliss!
But when we turned her sweet unlearnèd eye
On our own isle, she raised a joyous cry—
    "Oh! yes, I see it, Letty's home is there!"
    And while she hid all England with a kiss,
Bright over Europe fell her golden hair.

RICHARD CHENEVIX TRENCH
[1807-1886]

Gibraltar

ENGLAND, we love thee better than we know.—
  And this I learn'd when, after wand'rings long
  'Mid people of another stock and tongue,
I heard again thy martial music blow,
And saw thy gallant children to and fro
  Pace, keeping ward at one of those huge gates,
  Twin giants watching the Herculean Straits.
When first I came in sight of that brave show,
  It made the very heart within me dance,
  To think that thou thy proud foot shouldst advance
    Forward so far into the mighty sea.
Joy was it and exultation to behold
  Thine ancient standard's rich emblazonry,
  A glorious picture by the wind unroll'd.

AUBREY DE VERE
[1814-1902]

The Sun God

I SAW the Master of the Sun. He stood
  High in his luminous car, himself more bright;
  An Archer of immeasurable might:
On his left shoulder hung his quiver'd load;
Spurn'd by his steeds the eastern mountains glowed;
  Forward his eagle eye and bow of Light
He bent, and while both hands that arch embowed,
  Shaft after shaft pursued the flying night.
No wings profaned that godlike form: around
  His neck high held an ever-moving crowd
Of locks hung glistening: while such perfect sound
  Fell from his bowstring that th' ethereal dome
Thrilled as a dew-drop; and each passing cloud
  Expanded, whitening like the ocean foam.

MATTHEW ARNOLD
[1822-1888]

Austerity of Poetry

THAT son of Italy[1] who tried to blow,
Ere Dante came, the trump of sacred song,
In his light youth amid a festal throng
Sate with his bride to see a public show.
Fair was the bride, and on her front did glow
Youth like a star; and what to youth belong,
Gay raiment, sparkling gauds, elation strong.
A prop gave way! crash fell a platform! lo,
Mid struggling sufferers, hurt to death, she lay!
Shuddering they drew her garments off—and found
A robe of sackcloth next the smooth, white skin.
Such, poets, is your bride, the Muse! young, gay,
Radiant, adorn'd outside; a hidden ground
Of thought and of austerity within.

---

[1] [That son of Italy] Giacopone di Todi.

MATTHEW ARNOLD

Shakespeare

OTHERS abide our question. Thou art free.
We ask and ask: Thou smilest and art still,
Out-topping knowledge. For the loftiest hill
That to the stars uncrowns his majesty,
Planting his steadfast footsteps in the sea,
Making the heaven of heavens his dwelling-place,
Spares but the cloudy border of his base
To the foil'd searching of mortality;
And thou, who didst the stars and sunbeams know,
Self-school'd, self-scann'd, self-honour'd, self-secure,
Didst walk on earth unguess'd at. Better so!
All pains the immortal spirit must endure,
  All weakness that impairs, all griefs that bow,
  Find their sole voice in that victorious brow.

SYDNEY DOBELL

[1824-1874]

America

NOR force nor fraud shall sunder us! O ye
Who north or south, on east or western land,
Native to noble sounds, say truth for truth,
Freedom for freedom, love for love, and God
For God; Oh ye who in eternal youth
Speak with a living and creative flood
This universal English, and do stand
Its breathing book; live worthy of that grand
Heroic utterance—parted, yet a whole,
Far, yet unsever'd,—children brave and free
Of the great Mother-tongue, and ye shall be
Lords of an Empire wide as Shakespeare's soul,
Sublime as Milton's immemorial theme,
And rich as Chaucer's speech, and fair as Spenser's
    dream.

DANTE GABRIEL ROSSETTI
[1828-1882]

The Sonnet

A SONNET is a moment's monument,—
  Memorial from the Soul's eternity
  To one dead deathless hour. Look that it be,
Whether for lustral rite or dire portent,
Of its own arduous fulness reverent:
  Carve it in ivory or in ebony,
  As Day or Night may rule; and let Time see
Its flowering crest impearled and orient.
A Sonnet is a coin: its face reveals
  The soul,—its converse, to what Power 'tis due:—
Whether for tribute to the august appeals
  Of Life, or dower in Love's high retinue,
    It serve; or, 'mid the dark wharf's cavernous
      breath,
    In Charon's palm it pay the toll to Death.

DANTE GABRIEL ROSSETTI

Love Sight

WHEN do I see thee most, beloved one?
  When in the light the spirits of mine eyes
  Before thy face, their altar, solemnize
The worship of that love thro' thee made known?
Or when, in the dusk hours (we two alone),
  Close-kiss'd, and eloquent of still replies
  Thy twilight hidden glimmering visage lies,
And my soul only sees thy soul its own?
O love, my love! if I no more should see
Thyself, nor on the earth the shadow of thee,
  Nor image of thine eyes in any spring,—
How then should sound upon Life's darkening slope
The ground-whirl of the perish'd leaves of Hope,
  The wind of Death's imperishable wing?

DANTE GABRIEL ROSSETTI

Lost Days

THE lost days of my life until to-day,
  What were they, could I see them on the street
  Lie as they fell? Would they be ears of wheat
Sown once for food but trodden into clay?
Or golden coins squandered and still to pay?
  Or drops of blood dabbling the guilty feet?
  Or such spilt water as in dreams must cheat
The throats of men in Hell, who thirst alway?
I do not see them here; but after death
  God knows I know the faces I shall see,
Each one a murdered self, with low last breath,
  "I am thyself,—what hast thou done to me?"
"And I—and I—thyself," (lo! each one saith),
  "And thou thyself to all eternity!"

DANTE GABRIEL ROSSETTI

Refusal of Aid between Nations

Not that the earth is changing, O my God!
  Nor that the seasons totter in their walk,—
  Not that the virulent ill of act and talk
Seethes ever as a winepress ever trod,—
Not therefore are we certain that the rod
  Weighs in thine hand to smite the world; though
    now
  Beneath thine hand so many nations bow,
So many kings:—not therefore, O my God!—
But because Man is parcelled out in men
  Even thus; because, for any wrongful blow,
    No man not stricken asks, "I would be told
Why thou dost strike"; but his heart whispers then,
  "He is he, I am I." By this we know
    That the earth falls asunder, being old.

DANTE GABRIEL ROSSETTI

A Venetian Pastoral

WATER, for anguish of the solstice:—nay
   But dip the vessel slowly,—nay, but lean
   And hark how at its verge the wave sighs in
Reluctant. Hush! Beyond all depth away
The heat lies silent at the brink of day:
   Now the hand trails upon the viol-string
   That sobs, and the brown faces cease to sing,
Sad with the whole of pleasure. Whither stray
Her eyes now, from whose mouth the slim pipes
    creep
   And leave it pouting, while the shadowed grass
    Is cool against her naked side? Let be:—
Say nothing now unto her lest she weep,
   Nor name this ever. Be it as it was,—
    Life touching lips with Immortality.

GEORGE MEREDITH
[1828-1909]

Lucifer in Starlight

On a starr'd night Prince Lucifer uprose.
  Tired of his dark dominion swung the fiend
  Above the rolling ball in cloud part screen'd,
Where sinners hugged their spectre of repose.
Poor prey to his hot fit of pride were those.
  And now upon his western wing he leaned,
  Now his huge bulk o'er Afric's sands careened,
Now the black planet shadow'd Arctic snows.
Soaring through wider zones that pricked his scars
  With memory of the old revolt from Awe,
He reached a middle height, and at the stars,
Which are the brain of heaven, he looked, and sank.
Around the ancient track marched, rank on rank,
  The army of unalterable law.

JOHN LEICESTER WARREN
LORD DE TABLEY
[1835-1895]

The Two Old Kings

In ruling well what guerdon? Life runs low,
  As yonder lamp upon the hour-glass lies,
  Waning and wasted. We are great and wise,
But Love is gone; and Silence seems to grow
Along the misty road where we must go.
  From summits near the morning star's uprise
  Death comes, a shadow from the northern skies,
As, when all leaves are down, there comes the snow.
Brother and King, we hold our last carouse.
  One loving-cup we drain and then farewell.
    The night is spent: the crystal morning ray
Calls us, as soldiers laurell'd on our brows,
  To march undaunted while the clarions swell—
    Heroic hearts, upon our lonely way.

CHRISTINA GEORGINA ROSSETTI
[1830-1894]

Remember

REMEMBER me when I am gone away,
   Gone far away into the silent land;
   When you can no more hold me by the hand,
Nor I half turn to go, yet turning stay.
Remember me when no more day by day
   You tell me of our future that you planned:
   Only remember me; you understand
It will be late to counsel then or pray.
Yet if you should forget me for a while
   And afterwards remember, do not grieve:
   For if the darkness and corruption leave
   A vestige of the thoughts that once I had,
Better by far you should forget and smile
   Than that you should remember and be sad.

CHRISTINA GEORGINA ROSSETTI

Aloof

THE irresponsive silence of the land,
  The irresponsive sounding of the sea,
  Speak both one message of one sense to me:—
Aloof, aloof, we stand aloof, so stand
Thou too aloof, bound with the flawless band
  Of inner solitude; we bind not thee;
  But who from thy self-chain shall set thee free?
What heart shall touch thy heart? What hand thy
    hand?
And I am sometimes proud and sometimes meek,
  And sometimes I remember days of old
When fellowship seemed not so far to seek,
  And all the world and I seemed much less cold,
  And at the rainbow's foot lay surely gold,
And hope felt strong, and life itself not weak.

CHRISTINA GEORGINA ROSSETTI

Rest

O EARTH, lie heavily upon her eyes;
   Seal her sweet eyes weary of watching, Earth;
   Lie close around her; leave no room for mirth
With its harsh laughter, nor for sound of sighs.
She hath no questions, she hath no replies,
   Hush'd in and curtain'd with a blessèd dearth
   Of all that irked her from the hour of birth;
With stillness that is almost Paradise.
Darkness more clear than noonday holdeth her,
   Silence more musical than any song;
Even her very heart has ceased to stir:
Until the morning of Eternity
Her rest shall not begin nor end, but be;
   And when she wakes she will not think it long.

THOMAS HARDY
[1840-1928]

She, to Him

WHEN you shall see me in the toils of Time,
My lauded beauties carried off from me,
My eyes no longer stars as in their prime,
My name forgot of Maiden Fair and Free;
When in your being heart concedes to mind,
And judgment, though you scarce its process know,
Recalls the excellences I once enshrined,
And you are irk'd that they have withered so;
Remembering mine the loss is, not the blame,
That Sportsman Time but rears his brood to kill,
Knowing me in my soul the very same—
One who would die to spare you touch of ill!—
Will you not grant to old affection's claim
The hand of friendship down Life's sunless hill?

WILFRID SCAWEN BLUNT
[1840-1922]

St. Valentine's Day

To-DAY, all day, I rode upon the down,
With hounds and horsemen, a brave company:
On this side in its glory lay the sea,
On that the Sussex weald, a sea of brown.
The wind was light, and brightly the sun shone,
And still we gallop'd on from gorse to gorse:
And once, when check'd, a thrush sang, and my
    horse
Prick'd his quick ears as to a sound unknown.
I knew the Spring was come. I knew it even
Better than all by this, that through my chase
In bush and stone and hill and sea and heaven
I seem'd to see and follow still your face.
Your face my quarry was. For it I rode,
My horse a thing of wings, myself a god.

WILFRID SCAWEN BLUNT

Gibraltar

SEVEN weeks of sea, and twice seven days of storm
Upon the huge Atlantic, and once more
We ride into still water and the calm
Of a sweet evening, screen'd by either shore
Of Spain and Barbary. Our toils are o'er,
Our exile is accomplish'd. Once again
We look on Europe, mistress as of yore
Of the fair earth and of the hearts of men.
    Ay, this is the famed rock which Hercules
And Goth and Moor bequeath'd us. At this door
England stands sentry. God! to hear the shrill
Sweet treble of her fifes upon the breeze,
And at the summons of the rock gun's roar
To see her red coats marching from the hill!

MATHILDE BLIND
[1841-1896]

The Dead

THE dead abide with us. Though stark and cold
  Earth seem to grip them, they are with us still:
  They have forged our chains of being for good or ill,
And their invisible hands these hands yet hold.
Our perishable bodies are the mould
  In which their strong imperishable will—
  Mortality's deep yearning to fulfil—
Hath grown incorporate through dim time untold.
    Vibrations infinite of life in death,
  As a star's travelling light survives its star!
  So may we hold our lives that, when we are
    The fate of those who then will draw this breath,
  They shall not drag us to their judgment bar
    And curse the heritage that we bequeath.

ANDREW LANG
[1844-1912]

The Odyssey

As one that for a weary space has lain
  Lull'd by the song of Circe and her wine
  In gardens near the pale of Proserpine,
Where that Æean isle forgets the main,
And only the low lutes of love complain,
  And only shadows of wan lovers pine—
  As such an one were glad to know the brine
Salt on his lips, and the large air again,—
So gladly, from the songs of modern speech
  Men turn, and see the stars, and feel the free
    Shrill wind beyond the close of heavy flowers,
    And through the music of the languid hours
They hear like Ocean on the western beach
  The surge and thunder of the Odyssey.

EUGENE LEE-HAMILTON
[1845-1907]

Idle Charon

THE shores of Styx are lone for evermore,
　And not one shadowy form upon the steep
　Looms through the dusk, as far as eyes can sweep,
To call the ferry over as of yore;
But tintless rushes, all about the shore,
　Have hemm'd the old boat in, where, lock'd in
　　sleep,
　Hoar-bearded Charon lies; while pale weeds creep
With tightening grasp all round the unused oar.
For in the world of Life strange rumours run
　That now the Soul departs not with the breath,
But that the Body and the Soul are one;
　And in the loved one's mouth, now, after death,
The widow puts no obol, nor the son,
　To pay the ferry in the world beneath.

EDWARD CRACROFT LEFROY
[1855-1891]

The Flute of Daphnis

I AM the flute of Daphnis. On this wall
    He nail'd his tribute to the great god Pan,
What time he grew from boyhood, shapely, tall,
    And felt the first deep ardours of a man.
    Through adult veins more swift the song-tide ran,—
A vernal stream whose swollen torrents call
    For instant ease in utterance. Then began
That course of triumph reverenced by all.
Him the gods loved, and more than other men
    Blessed with the flower of beauty, and endowed
His soul of music with the strength of ten.
    Now on a festal day I see the crowd
Look fondly at my resting-place, and when
    I think whose lips have press'd me, I am proud.

MARGARET L. WOODS
[*b.* 1856]

Genius Loci

PEACE, Shepherd, peace! What boots it singing on?
  Since long ago grace-giving Phœbus died,
    And all the train that loved the stream-bright side
Of the poetic mount with him are gone
Beyond the shores of Styx and Acheron,
  In unexplorèd realms of night to hide.
    The clouds that strew their shadows far and wide
Are all of Heaven that visits Helicon.

Yet here, where never muse or god did haunt,
  Still may some nameless power of Nature stray,
Pleased with the reedy stream's continual chant
  And purple pomp of these broad fields in May.
The shepherds meet him where he herds the kine,
And careless pass him by whose is the gift divine.

ALICE MEYNELL
[1850-1922]

Renouncement

I MUST not think of thee; and, tired yet strong,
  I shun the love that lurks in all delight—
  The love of thee—and in the blue heaven's height,
And in the dearest passage of a song.
Oh, just beyond the fairest thoughts that throng
  This breast, the thought of thee waits hidden yet
    bright;
  But it must never, never come in sight;
I must stop short of thee the whole day long.

But when sleep comes to close each difficult day,
  When night gives pause to the long watch I keep,
    And all my bonds I needs must loose apart,
Must doff my will as raiment laid away,—
  With the first dream that comes with the first sleep
    I run, I run, I am gather'd to thy heart.

GERARD MANLEY HOPKINS
[1844-1898]

The Immanent

As kingfishers catch fire, dragonflies draw flame;
As tumbled over rim in roundy wells
Stones ring; like each tucked string tells, each hung
    bell's
Bow swung finds tongue to fling out broad its name;
Each mortal thing does one thing and the same;
Deals out that being indoors each one dwells;
Selves—goes itself; *myself* it speaks and spells,
Crying *What I do is me; for that I came.*

I say more: the just man justices;
Keeps grace: that keeps all his goings graces;
Acts in God's eyes what in God's eye he is—
Christ—for Christ plays in ten thousand places,
Lovely in limbs, and lovely in eyes not his
To the Father through the features of men's faces.

GERARD MANLEY HOPKINS

Abyss

No worst, there is none. Pitched past pitch of grief,
More pangs will, schooled at forepangs, wilder wring.
Comforter, where, where is your comforting?
Mary, mother of us, where is your relief?
My cries heave, herds-long; huddle in a main, a chief
Woe, world-sorrow; on an age-old anvil wince and
    sing—
Then lull, then leave off. Fury had shrieked "No ling-
ering. Let me be fell: force I must be brief."

O the mind, mind has mountains; cliffs of fall
Frightful, sheer, no-man-fathomed. Hold them cheap
May who ne'er hung there. Nor does long our small
Durance deal with that steep or deep. Here! creep,
Wretch, under a comfort serves in a whirlwind: all
Life death does end and each day dies with sleep.

WILLIAM WATSON
[1858-1935]

So, without overt breach, we fall apart,
Tacitly sunder—neither you nor I
Conscious of one intelligible Why,
And both, from severance, winning equal smart.
So, with resigned and acquiescent heart,
Whene'er your name on some chance lip may lie,
I seem to see an alien shade pass by,
A spirit wherein I have no lot or part.

Thus may a captive, in some fortress grim,
From casual speech betwixt his warders, learn
That June on her triumphant progress goes
Through arched and bannered woodlands; while for
    him
She is a legend emptied of concern,
And idle is the rumour of the rose.

LORD ALFRED DOUGLAS
[*b.* 1870]

Impression de Nuit
London

SEE what a mass of gems the city wears
Upon her broad live bosom! row on row
Rubies and emeralds and amethysts glow.
See that huge circle like a necklace, stares
With thousands of bold eyes to heaven, and dares
The golden stars to dim the lamps below,
And in the mirror of the mire I know
The moon has left her image unawares.

That's the great town at night: I see her breasts,
Pricked out with lamps they stand like huge black
    towers,
I think they move! I hear her panting breath.
And that's her head where the tiara rests.
And in her brain, through lanes as dark as death,
Men creep like thoughts . . . the lamps are like pale
    flowers.

LORD ALFRED DOUGLAS

The Wastes of Time

IF you came back, perhaps you would not find
The old enchantment, nor again discern
The altered face of love. The wheels yet turn
That clocked the wasted hours, the spirit's wind
Still fans the embers in the hidden mind.
But if I cried to you, "Return! return!"
How could you come? How could you ever learn
The old ways you have left so far behind?

How sweetly, forged in sleep, come dreams that make
Swift wings and ships that sail the estranging sea,
Less roughly than blown rose-leaves in a bowl,
To harboured bliss. But oh! the pain to wake
In empty night seeking what may not be
Till the dead flesh set free the living soul.

JOHN MASEFIELD

Poet Laureate

[*b.* 1875]

Roses

Roses are beauty, but I never see
Those blood-drops from the burning heart of June
Glowing like thought upon the living tree
Without a pity that they die so soon,
Die into petals, like those roses old,
Those women, who were summer in men's hearts
Before the smile upon the Sphinx was cold
Or sand had hid the Syrian and his arts.
O myriad dust of beauty that lies thick
Under our feet and not a single grain
But stirred and moved in beauty and was quick
For one brief moon and died nor lived again;
But when the moon rose lay upon the grass
Pasture to living beauty, life that was.

RUPERT BROOKE
[1887-1915]

The Dead

THESE hearts were woven of human joys and cares,
Washed marvellously with sorrow, swift to mirth.
The years had given them kindness. Dawn was theirs,
And sunset and the colours of the earth.
These had seen movement, and heard music; known
Slumber and waking; loved; gone proudly friended;
Felt the quick stir of wonder; sat alone;
Touched flowers and furs, and cheeks. All this is
    ended.
There are waters blown by changing winds to laughter
And lit by the rich skies, all day. And after,
Frost, with a gesture, stays the waves that dance
And wandering loveliness. He leaves a white
Unbroken glory, a gathered radiance,
A width, a shining peace, under the night.

RUPERT BROOKE

The Soldier

IF I should die, think only this of me:
That there's some corner of a foreign field
That is for ever England. There shall be
In that rich earth a richer dust concealed;
A dust whom England bore, shaped, made aware,
Gave, once, her flowers to love, her ways to roam,
A body of England's, breathing English air,
Washed by the rivers, blest by suns of home.
And think, this heart, all evil shed away,
A pulse in the eternal mind, no less
Gives somewhere back the thoughts by England given;
Her sights and sounds; dreams happy as her day;
And laughter, learnt of friends; and gentleness,
In hearts at peace, under an English heaven.

WILFRED OWEN
[1895-1918]

Anthem for Doomed Youth

WHAT passing-bells for those who die as cattle?
Only the monstrous anger of the guns.
Only the stuttering rifles' rapid rattle
Can patter out their hasty orisons.
No mockeries for them from prayers or bells,
Nor any voice of mourning save the choirs,—
The shrill, demented choirs of wailing shells;
And bugles calling for them from sad shires.

What candles may be held to speed them all?
Not in the hands of boys, but in their eyes
Shall shine the holy glimmers of good-byes.
The pallor of girls' brows shall be their pall;
Their flowers the tenderness of silent minds,
And each slow dusk a drawing-room of blinds.

WILFRED OWEN

The End

AFTER the blast of lightning from the East,
The flourish of long clouds, the Chariot Throne;
After the drums of Time have rolled and ceased,
And by the bronze west long retreat is blown,

Shall life renew these bodies? Of a truth
All Death will He annul, all tears assuage?—
Fill the void veins of Life again with youth,
And wash, with an immortal water, Age?

When I do ask white Age he saith not so:
"My head hangs weighed with snow."
And when I hearken to the Earth, she saith:
"My fiery heart shrinks, aching. It is death.
Mine ancient scars shall not be glorified,
Nor my titanic tears, the seas, be dried."

ROBERT GITTINGS
[*b*. 1915]

Parting

I SHALL not see you for a hundred days:
A quarter of a year to watch my heart,
Be patient and put down the voice which says,
"It is a kind of death to be apart":
Take up acquaintances, lay quite aside
Love's inward study, give desire a fee
To buy philosophy and so to abide
Time, distance, and the white, departing sea.
Only a fool believes that memory
Can pension off the past. That you are gone
I know; I must endure it, that I know;
But how or why, except by love alone,
Goes beyond reasoning. Yet we two shall lie
At one to-night if both shall wish it so.

NOTES

Page 5. "Prometheus, when first from heaven high."
In line 3 the printed copies (including that in *England's Helicon*, 1600) give "fond of delight." "Fond of the light" is Dr. Hannah's correction, from the Harleian MS. For the fancy of this sonnet, cf. Herrick, *Hesperides*, 565:

> "I played with Love, as with the fire
>   The wanton Satyr did;
> Nor did I know, or could descry
>   What under these was hid.
> That Satyr he but burnt his lips;
>   But mine's the greater smart,
> For kissing Love's dissembling chips
>   The fire scorched my heart."

Page 7. "Happy ye leaves whenas those lily hands."
The lady of the sonnet—the Elizabeth whom Spenser married in Ireland on St. Barnabas' Day, 1594, and for whom he wrote his magnificent *Epithalamion*—was almost certainly Elizabeth Boyle, of Kilcoran by the Bay of Youghal, a kinswoman of the great Earl of Cork. Dr. Grosart (*Complete Works in Verse and Prose of Edmund Spenser*, vol. i.) has discovered a grant, made in 1606 by Sir Richard Boyle to Elizabeth Boyle, *alias* Seckerstone, widow, of her house at Kilcoran for half-a-crown a year. Now it is known that Spenser's widow married one Roger Seckerstone in 1603; and it is, to say the least, unlikely

NOTES

that there were two Elizabeth Seckerstones (unusual name!) in the neighbourhood at one time.

"Of *Helicon*, whence she derivèd is"—cf. Sonnet, p. 11, line 10: "My *Helice*, the lodestar of my life." *Helice*, it is suggested, stands for Elisé, Elizabeth.

Page 15. "One day I wrote her name upon the strand." See note preceding. The strand of Kilcoran—three miles long—is famous.

Page 20. "With how sad steps, O moon, thou climb'st the skies!" "The last line of this poem," says Charles Lamb, "is a little obscured by transposition. He means, 'Do they call ungratefulness there a virtue?' "

Page 35. This sonnet of Daniel palely imitates and faintly echoes a famous one by Pierre de Ronsard:

Quand vous serez bien vielle, un soir, à la chandelle,
  Assise auprès du feu, devidant et filant,
Direz chantant mes vers, en vous esmerveillant;
  Ronsard me celebrait du temps que j'étais belle.

Lors vous n'aurez servante ayant telle nouvelle,
  Desja sous le labeur à demy sommeillant,
Qui a bruit de mon nom ne s'aille resveillant,
  Benissant vostre nom de lonange immortelle.

Je seray sous la terre, et, fantasme sans os,
  Par les ombres mysteux je prendray mon repos;
Vous serez au fouyer une vieele accroupie,

Regrettant mon amour et vostre fier desdain,
  Vivez, si m'en croyez, n'attendez à demain
Cueillez des aujord'huy les roses de la vie.

NOTES

Ronsard's beautiful opening has started many poets, and Mr. W. B. Yeats in our day has pursued it to a fine issue of his own in a lyric beginning:

> When you are old and grey and full of sleep
> And, nodding by the fire, take down this book. . . .

Page 53. "Full many a glorious morning have I seen." I suppose that in the last line ("Suns of the world may stain when heaven's sun staineth") "stain" = "be stained"—*i.e.* with clouds. But the context seems to suggest that "stain" may stand for " 'stain," "abstain."

Page 91. "Captain or Colonel, or Knight in Arms." The date "when the assault was intended"—or at least expected—"to the city" was Nov. 13, 1642. After Edgehill (Oct. 23) the Royal army advanced up the Thames valley upon London; took Brentford on Nov. 12; and on the following day advanced as far as Turnham Green, and were met by the Parliamentarians, 24,000 strong. The two armies "stood many hours in battalia facing one another." It seems to have been a case of "one was afraid and t'other didn't dare." In the end the Royal army, which was short of ammunition, withdrew to Colnbrook.

"The great Emathian conqueror"—Alexander the Great, who was said (see Mr. Mark Pattison's note for authorities) to have spared Pindar's house at the sack of Thebes, 333 B.C. Emathian = Macedonian.

"Sad Electra's poet"—Euripides. Milton's authority here is Plutarch, who tells that when the Lacedæmonians took Athens in 404 B.C. they were incited by the Thebans to raze the city to the ground. The decision was in suspense when, as the generals sat at wine together, a Phocian sang part of the chorus from the *Electra*, which so affected all present that they agreed at once it would be an unworthy act to destroy a city that had given birth to such poetry.

Page 93. "Daughter to that good Earl, once President." The Lady Margaret Ley was daughter of James Ley (1552-1629), made Lord High Treasurer in 1622, Lord President of the Council in 1628, and in that same year advanced to the earldom of Scarborough. His death coincided with the sudden breaking up of the third Parliament of Charles I, and is compared by Milton with the death of the Athenian orator, Isocrates ("that old man eloquent"), after the battle of Chæronea, 338 B.C., when Philip of Macedon destroyed the combined forces of Athens and Thebes. Isocrates (he was in his 99th year, by the way) died four days after receiving the news of Chæronea, just as Ley died four days after the dissolution of Parliament on March 10, 1629.

Page 94. "Harry, whose tuneful and well-measured song." Henry Lawes, of the Chapel Royal, was Milton's friend from boyhood. He dedicated his book, *Choice Psalmes*, in 1648, to King Charles, then a captive. "It was this Royalist and Cavalier volume to which Milton supplied the recommendatory sonnet. Violent partisan as Milton was he did not allow political feeling to sever the tie of early friendship, or of a common love of musical art."—*Pattison*. Line 4—"committing short and long." Lat. *committere*, to pair, to set together.

NOTES

Page 96. "Cromwell, our chief of men, who through a cloud." Not a general testimony to Cromwell's character, but addressed to him on a special emergency. "The moment was one when the question of a 'maintenance for a godley ministry' was the uppermost question. The Presbyterian party, especially in London and Lancashire, wanted a state-supported church and tithes, or a provision in lieu of tithes, while the Independent party regarded with aversion any interference of the secular arm with spiritual things. The extreme view, shared by Milton, went so far as to look upon payment for spiritual ministration as contrary to the gospel."—*Pattison*.

The "Committee for the Propagation of the Gospel" was a committee of the Rump Parliament, fourteen in number, having general supervision of church affairs, and, in particular, the duty of providing spiritual food for destitute parishes. To this committee "certain ministers," headed by John Owen, had offered fifteen Proposals, in which they asked that preachers should receive a public maintenance.

Line 14. "Whose Gospel is their maw"—cf. *Lycidas* (written in 1637):

"How well could I have spared for thee, young swain,
  Enow of such as for their bellies' sake,
  Creep, and intrude, and climb into the fold!
  Of other care they little reckoning make,
  Than how to scramble at the shearer's feast,
  And shove away the worthy bidden guest.
  Blind mouths! . . . ."

NOTES

Page 97. "Vane, young in years, but in sage counsel old." Sir Henry Vane, the younger, born in 1612, and therefore forty years old at the date of this sonnet, was the son of Sir Henry Vane, of Raby Castle, county Durham. He was governor of Massachusetts in 1636, but soon returned to England, entered Parliament, and was appointed Treasurer of the Navy. He took an active part against Strafford, and was principal mover of the Covenant in England and the Self-denying Ordinance. Although not a regicide, he suffered death on that ground in 1662.

Line 4. "The fierce Epirot" is Pyrrhus, repelled 279 B.C.; and "the African bold," Hannibal. Pattison quotes Duruy, *Histoire des Romaines*, as saying of Hannibal in 203 B.C., "il se sentait vaincu par quelque chose de plus fort que son génie, les mœurs et les institutions de Rome."

Page 98. "Avenge, O Lord, thy slaughtered saints, whose bones." In Jan. 1655 the Duke of Savoy determined to make the poor Vaudois inhabitants of certain Piedmontese valleys renounce the simple forms of faith and worship they had inherited from days long before Luther, and conform to the Catholic religion. They remonstrated; and in April 1655 a crowd of hired soldiery poured into the valleys and revelled there for many days in rape, pillage, and savage massacre. The news took nearly a month to reach England; but when it came "a cry of horror went through the country. . . . A day of humiliation was appointed, large collections were made for the sufferers, and a special envoy was despatched to remonstrate with the Duke of Savoy." The government despatches in this business were written by Milton.

Lines 7, 8. "that rolled Mother with infant down the rocks"—"A mother was hurled down a mighty rock with a little infant in her arms; and three days after was found dead with the child alive, but fast claspt between the arms of the mother, which were cold and stiff, insomuch that those that found them had much ado to get the child out."—*Account of the massacre by Sir William Moreland, Cromwell's Agent in Piedmont: published in 1658.*

Page 100. "Lawrence, of virtuous father virtuous son" —cf. Horace, *Carm.*, line 16, "O matre pulchra filia pulchrior." The Lawrence addressed was one of the sons of Henry Lawrence, President of the Council in 1654.

Page 101. "Cyriack, whose grandsire on the royal bench." The mother of Cyriack Skinner was Bridget, a daughter of the famous Sir Edward Coke.

Page 102. "Cyriack, this three years' day these eyes, though clear." The allusion in lines 10-12 is to the *Defensio pro populo Anglicano contra Salmasium*, which Milton had persisted in writing, though warned by the physician of the probable consequences to his eyesight.

Page 103. "Methought I saw my late espousèd saint." Milton on Nov. 12, 1656, married Catherine Woodcock, daughter of Captain Woodcock, of Hackney. After fifteen months of married happiness, she died in child-bed, February 1658, her baby surviving but a month.

NOTES

Page 105. "Cambridge, with whom, my pilot and my guide"—Richard Owen Cambridge (1717-1802), now chiefly memorable as the author of *The Scribleriad* (1751).

Line 2. "Pleased I have traversed thy Sabrina's flood." Cambridge resided at Whitminster in Gloucestershire, close to the Severn, and on the banks of the Stroud which runs into that river. Cf. Chalmers' Memoir: "While he continued to cultivate polite literature, his more active hours were employed in heightening the beauties of the scenery around his seat; for this purpose he made the little river Stroud navigable for some distance, and not only constructed boats for pleasure or carriage, but introduced some ingenious improvements in that branch of naval architecture, which were approved by the most competent judges."—*Chalmers' English Poets*, vol. 18, p. 227.

Pages 112-13. "It was the candle of Bowles that lit the fire of Coleridge," says Mr. Austin Dobson. In a copy of the *Sonnets* (first published in 1789) preserved at South Kensington, Coleridge writes of them as "having done his heart more good than all the other books he ever read excepting his Bible." They have now an historical rather than an intrinsic interest.

Page 119. "Toussaint, the most unhappy man of men!" François Dominique Toussaint l'Ouverture, son of African slaves, was born in San Domingo, 1743; appointed chief of the army of San Domingo by the Directory in 1796, and ruled the island with justice and vigour. In 1801, when Bonaparte sought to restore slavery

in San Domingo, Toussaint resisted, but was compelled
to surrender, and was sent to France, where he died in
prison (1803).

Page 132. "Tax not the royal Saint with vain ex-
pense." The royal Saint is Henry VI. This favourite (but
to my mind much over-rated) sonnet is taken, together
with "Walton's Book of Lives" and "Mutability," from
the Ecclesiastical Sonnets, part iii (1822).

Page 144. "O lift with reverent hand that tarnished
flower." "In a leaf of a quarto edition of the *Lives of the
Saints*, written in Spanish by the learned and reverend
father, Alfonso Villegas, Divine, of the Order of St.
Dominick, set forth in English by John Heigham, Anno
1630, bought at a Catholic book-shop in Duke Street,
Lincoln's Inn Fields, I found, carefully inserted, a painted
flower, seemingly coeval with the book itself; and did not,
for some time, discover that it opened in the middle, and
was the cover to a very humble draught of a St. Anne,
with the Virgin and Child; doubtless the performance
of some poor but pious Catholic, whose meditations it
assisted."—*Lamb's Note*.

Page 145. "Mysterious Night! when our first parent
knew." According to Coleridge "the finest and most
grandly conceived sonnet in our language"; and accord-
ing to Leigh Hunt, "Supreme, perhaps, above all in any
language; nor can we ponder it too deeply, or with too
hopeful a reverence."

Blanco White's "Night and Death" is now the
classical instance of a man's attaining to enduring
poetic fame by a single sonnet. It is not that the rest of
his writings fell far below, but that practically he

NOTES

exhausted himself with this one great stroke, and wrote no more. The largest information on "Night and Death" (which has quite a literature of its own) will be found in Mr. David M. Main's *Treasury of English Sonnets.*

Page 146. "Green little vaulter in the sunny grass." Written in friendly rivalry with Keats, whose sonnet on the same subject will be found on p. 157.

Page 147. "It flows through old hushed Ægypt and its sands." This, too, was written in friendly competition —with Keats and Shelley. To my mind, Hunt fairly worsted Keats in the *Grasshopper and Cricket* sonnet; but there can be no doubt at all that with his sonnet on the Nile he bore the palm away from the two greater poets. Here are the rival sonnets:

"Month after month the gathering rains descend,
   Drenching yon secret Ethiopian dells,
   And from the desert's ice-girt pinnacles
Where frost and heat in strange embraces blend
On Atlas, fields of moist snow half depend.
   Girt these with blasts and meteors, Tempest dwells
   By Nile's aerial urn; with rapid spells
Urging those waters to their mighty end.
O'er Egypt's land of memory floods are level
   And they are thine, O Nile—and well thou knowest
That soul-sustaining airs and blasts of evil
   And fruits and poisons spring where'er thou flowest.
Beware, O Man—for knowledge must to thee
Like the great flood to Egypt ever be."—*Shelley.*

NOTES

"Son of the old moon-mountains African!
   Chief of the Pyramid and Crocodile!
   We call thee fruitful, and, that very while,
A desert fills one seeing 's inward span;
Nurse of swart nations since the world began,
   Art thou so fruitful? Or dost thou beguile
   Such men to honour thee, who, worn with toil,
Rest for a space 'twixt Cairo and Decan?
O may dark fancies err! they surely do;
   'Tis ignorance that makes a barren waste
Of all beyond itself; thou dost bedew
   Green rushes like our rivers, and dost taste
The pleasant sun-rise; green isles hast thou too,
   And to the sea as happily dost haste."—*Keats*.

Page 156. "Much have I travelled in the realms of gold." Cowden Clarke records that in his lodgings at Clerkenwell, one night in the summer of 1815, he and Keats sat together till daylight over a borrowed folio copy of Chapman's Homer; and that, when he came down to breakfast, at ten o'clock next morning, he received this now famous sonnet which Keats had found time to compose and send from the Borough.

Line 11. "Cortez" is of course a mistake. The discoverer of the Pacific was Vasco Nuñez de Balboa, and the date of the discovery, 1513.

Page 157. "The poetry of earth is never dead"—see note on Leigh Hunt's sonnet, *supra*.

INDEX OF FIRST LINES

226

INDEX OF FIRST LINES

INDEX OF FIRST LINES

INDEX OF FIRST LINES

INDEX OF FIRST LINES

INDEX OF FIRST LINES

INDEX OF FIRST LINES